The Foundation For Missions

M. Thomas Starkes

BROADMAN PRESS
Nashville, Tennessee

© Copyright 1981 • Broadman Press.
All rights reserved.

4263-25

ISBN: 0-8054-6325-9

Dewey Decimal Classification: 266
Subject heading: MISSIONS
Library of Congress Catalog Card Number: 80-67460
Printed in the United States of America

Preface

The Bible is the textbook for modern missions. It speaks with clarity while sounding a clarion call to participation in what God is doing in his world.

However, sometimes the "thees, thous, and therefores" of the Bible pile up so high that its ability to speak to everyone becomes clouded. This devotional book is written to try to eliminate that cloud. Each chapter is designed to speak clearly to the lay reader in everyday terms.

With clear communication in mind and with profound reverence to the Bible, each chapter is followed by an addendum in modern language. These are designed to capture for the earth dweller of the 1980s a portion of Scripture.

My father was a man of limited education, but had a deep love for the Bible. He hardly missed a day reading it after his initial commitment to Jesus, his Lord. To him and all of like mind, this work is dedicated.

M. Thomas Starkes

Contents

Introduction

One of Paul's greatest metaphors is that of the church as a building. This is an expression he uses often in 1 and 2 Corinthians and Romans. He phrases his thesis very succinctly in 1 Corinthians 3:11, "For no other foundation can any one lay than that which is laid, which is Jesus Christ" (RSV).

Successful life-builders today, regardless of cultural background, build on the foundation of Christ. In Galatians 1:6-7, Paul makes it clear that the one foundation of the church is Jesus Christ and his gospel. He writes, "I marvel that ye are so soon removed from him that called you into the grace of Christ into another gospel: which is not another; but there be some that trouble you, and would pervert the gospel of Christ."

Paul, the church's greatest missionary evangelist and theologian since Christ, knew that no other person or idea, not even Simon Peter, can be the central building stone of the church. It is Paul's clear stance in all his letters that no revelation or philosophy apart from Christ is adequate as a foundation for the church.

Paul goes on in the verses which follow that since Christ is the church's foundation, persons who follow him with varying talents may add to the church's fellowship and ministry by building on that foundation alone. Anytime a church attempts missions and ministry on any other base, it is doomed to failure.

This book is entitled *The Foundation for Missions* and is based on the truth that Christ is the center of the cause of missions. It is based also on the idea that missions is not only what we adore, but what we do and say. As a devotional guide, this book is designed to lead to action. Prayer and piety are never intended in the church as ends in themselves. Even those who pray "the Lord of the harvest" are to do so "that he will send forth labourers" (Matt. 9:38). Devotion and deed are twin actors in the task of missions.

If anyone in his day knew that fact, it was Paul. He stayed on the move, carrying his rich and deep devotional life with him. For example, when he went from Troas to Philippi, he met and baptized Lydia. He was first attracted to her because he had heard that she was a woman of prayer and a believer in God (Acts 16:11-15). A group in Philippi customarily met for prayer outside the city gates near the Gangites River. The Greek word for prayer, *proseuche*, was frequently used by Hellenistic Jews as a synonym for synagogue. Lydia's group, along with Paul, knew that God could be worshiped anywhere, even while doing missions. They knew that devotion produced deeds.

Lydia listened to what Paul had to say. She and her whole household became Paul's first converts in the city of Philippi. They were all baptized. Paul's devotion on the move produced results. *The Foundation for Missions* provides help for that active style of devotion.

That missions began in the heart of God is clearly demonstrated in the shared beliefs of the worldwide Christian community. In the early 1980s, Christianity fights for survival, particularly in the triangular match between Communism and Islam. In 1981, the number *10* may represent Communism for there are ten hundred million, or one billion persons currently living under Communist domination. The number *9* may represent Christianity for there are nine hundred million Christians in the world, eight hundred million which are Roman Catholics. The number *8* may represent Islam for there are now about eight hundred million Muslims in the world. In the midst of this monumental challenge, Christians continue to virtually ignore Jesus' prayer that "they all might be one" and continue to squabble. Christ's followers argued over how to receive grace and sacramentalize that moment. We debate how to worship and what kind of buildings to worship in and when to worship. Christians fight over whether to use music, what kind to use, and when.

There are kernels of truth on which almost all Christians agree.

This is a clear sign that missions began and rests near to the heart of God; for these truths have managed to escape almost unscathed when the debating dust has cleared.

First, most Christians agree that there was a historical figure named Jesus of Nazareth and far more is known about him than other major world religion founders such as Buddha, Zoraster, or Confucius. Jesus' story is told in the Four Gospels, all dating from the same century he lived and arguing on the basic details of his life. It is written that Jesus was born about 5 BC and that his miraculous birth did not remove the necessity of child-rearing placed on his earthly parents, Joseph and Mary. While little is known of Jesus' childhood, it is assumed that he learned to read Hebrew and understood Greek, but his native language was that of Galilee, Aramaic. It is also indicated that Joseph died when Jesus was a teenager. Jesus was left to be the father figure for four other boys and at least two sisters. This he did until he was about thirty years of age.

When Jesus began his public ministry, it immediately was apparent that he was a popular preacher. His audiences were composed of rich and poor, powerful and powerless, the learned and the ignorant. His reputation soon spread as a friend of sinners. Jesus even considered women and children as capable of learning in time when education was strictly male-oriented. His teachings were augmented by healing and miracles.

After two and a half years of teaching in the north of Galilee, Jesus came to Jerusalem for his final days. There he went through several illegal trials and was sentenced to die. He was then executed by Roman crucifixion outside the city walls of Jerusalem.

Unlike other religious prophets, Jesus' story does not end there. A man named Joseph of Arimathaea, a member of the Jewish Council, buried the body of Jesus in his new rock tomb. Those closest to Jesus gave up hope. They refused to believe it three days later when they were told that Jesus was still alive. They were convinced when he appeared to them in private and to five hundred at once. Faith in the newly resurrected Lord turned the disciples from depression to triumph.

Today, almost two millenia later, Christ's followers are fragmented. There are more than one thousand identifiable sects and denominations dividing Christendom as it enters the 1980s. There are more than three hundred identifiable Christian denominations in the United States alone. Christians continue to fragment for political, ethnic, social, and doctrinal reasons. In spite of all these divisions, there are essential common strands of belief through all of them. They include:

1. **God.** God is seen by Christians to be the cause and ultimate source of this world. The first five words of the English Bible, "In the beginning God created ..." (Gen. 1:1), remain the foundation of Christian missions. The same holy and eternal God who was later to send Jesus of Nazareth as his clearest revelation, began it all by creating reality from his essence. He immediately revealed himself as a person who lives, cares, redeems, and creates. From the moment of creation, God has been a God of initiative, seeking to reveal himself to all who will heed.

The New Testament makes it clear that the work of creation was not that of the Father alone. The first eighteen verses of the Gospel of John make Jesus a partner in creation. In Colossians 1, Paul places Jesus in the center of creating and sustaining the entire universe. Therefore, Christians agree that Jesus does more than die for the human family. He holds all that is together on a continuing basis. Jesus Christ, as the solid foundation of missions, is also the foundation for all of life. This fact makes it clear that to proclaim and exemplify Jesus is to present reality for all that exists, not simply a white or Western faith. The surety of missions rests on the surety of all that is, has been, or will be.

2. **Mankind.** Christians agree that humans were created as the highest of God's creatures, but given absolute freedom which they constantly abuse. As the result of this abuse, humans worldwide stand in constant need of a reinstatement of status before the fall. Therefore, humans live in the tension of searching for good while doing evil. Modern Christians can identify with twentieth-century Christian martyr Dietrich Bonhoeffer, who wrote:

Who am I? This or the other?
Am I one person today and tomorrow another?

Am I both at once? A hypocrite before others?
And before myself a contemptibly woebegone weakling?
Or is something within me still like a beaten army?
Fleeing in disorder from the victory already achieved?[1]

While Christians agonize over their self-identify, they have seen an obvious clue to their potential in Jesus of Nazareth. Mankind was never to be the same again after Jesus became one of us. His brief earthly span indicates that humanity can never again be demeaned without injuring him personally. The one doing missions is hereafter dedicated to doing what Jesus did; that is, bringing deliverance to those captive of sin and oppression. Missions is, as Jesus did, enfleshing redemption for fellow humans.

3. **The Bible.** Christians worldwide argue that the Bible is the Word of God, a record of God's dealings with humans in history. It is agreed that the Bible was produced by God through a community of faith. In return, this community of faith, currently called the church, owes its existence to the Bible. The Bible today stands as a guidebook to the Christian life. It reveals the principles of missions to those who would do the bidding of its author. God's justice and love are thus experienced through the church to the world.

Born-again believers, knowing Jesus of Nazareth to be the living Word, see a qualitative difference between him and the written Word. While both are indispensable revelations of God, only Jesus is God himself. It is he who as God serves as the foundation of missions. This does not reduce the importance of the Bible's record of God's acts and intentions, however. These twin revelations serve as the foci of the book.

4. **The World.** With Christ Jesus as its foundation, the world was made by him and reclaimed by his earthly visit. This world, most Christians assert, was made by God and pronounced "good." It continues to exist as a testimony to the goodness and power of the One who made it. Yet, God allows sin and evil to exist in the world. He allows evil to exist because he allows human freedom. Further, there is an overriding natural law that God employs to govern the universe. Persons alive today go against this law only to their own defeat. They were given dominion over this world to use

it for their own good and ideally for the glory of God. God, in his wisdom, will not allow his final plan for the world to be defeated. Thus, anyone actively engaged in Christian missions is enfleshing the truth that God is still in ultimate control of human events, both present and future. When we act as missionaries, we are living testimonies that God, in his wisdom and power, will not allow his final plan for the world to be defeated. It is he who will write the final word on the final page of history and rule the world. When the missionary ministers, he does so in a world which is God's. Christ at the right hand of the Father is co-ruler and final determiner of the world's fate.

The great theologian, Karl Barth, met with a group of five outstanding Southern Baptist evangelists at his home just before his death. After conversing for two hours, one of the evangelists asked, as Karl led them to the door, whether this great thinker had a final word for them. "Yes," he said, "go and tell the world it is not lost." That is the message of missions. This world is not lost because it has never quite been the same since Jesus came, showing forever that to be a part of this is a godly thing.

5. **Eternity.** For most Christians alive in the 1980s, the culmination of salvation is the final blessing and abiding state of the redeemed. This is usually called heaven. Hell exists for those who reject the will of God for their lives and choose instead to live in a state of rebellion against him. The worst aspect of hell will be an absence from Christ, the foundation of eternal life itself. Believers, on the other hand, can emphasize and enjoy the sure promises of Christ regarding that quality of life called eternal. One such promise is found in John 11:25-26, "I am the resurrection, and the life: he that believeth in me, though he were dead, yet shall he live: And whosoever liveth and believeth in me shall never die." Yet, the Christian knows that there is another sense in which eternal life is a quality that begins "in the now" with acts of faith in God through Christ.

6. **The Church.** All Christians agree that the church is important for such functions as participating in the sacraments, worship, fellowship, teaching, ministering through social service, ministry, and

missionizing. Opinions may differ over a theoretical definition of the church, but there is a major agreement in the Christian community over its functional definition.

Most Christians agree that there is no task of Christians more dependent on the strength of the church than Christian missions. It is the church's resources, organization, prayer support, finances, and persevering power that provide missions with its staying dynamic. With Christ as its foundation, the church is the dominant energy base for the mission task.

7. **The Kingdom.** Christians through the past two millenia correctly have observed that the primary theme of Jesus' preaching was the kingdom of God. He repeatedly stated that the kingdom has several surprise elements which makes Christ's reign different from the normal cultural standards of value in the world. For example, Jesus taught that the kingdom belongs to the powerless and those who never suspect that they are a part of it. The normal standards by which the world judges success (money, fame, and power) are the kingdom's antagonists. This emphasis gives a unique flavor to Christian ethics and missions in their purest forms. When any Christian is involved in missions, he joins with God in upsetting the world's standards. At the same time, he is molding those standards in the image of Christ, the foundation of missions.

8. **Jesus Christ.** It is in Jesus, the Christ, that God shows himself to be a person with the obvious attributes of love, holiness, and involvement. Christians agree that to behold Jesus is to see God in a qualitative dimension not available in any other revelation. Christians worldwide assert that to see God in Christ is to see him in a way not possible elsewhere.

The Christ-event in Jesus of Nazareth is God's clearest revelation of himself. Anyone in the world who has chosen a revelation of God as truth for him (whether it be in a book or a person) should compare that revelation with Jesus.

There are eight qualities of Jesus that combine to rank him far above would-be usurpers of his throne at the right hand of the Father. They are:

(1) *Miraculous birth.*—What could not possibly happen did hap-

pen in Jesus of Nazareth: the one true God became a human being. One night a Jewish teenage peasant girl lay down and gave birth to a screaming, red-faced youngster and they called him *Emmanuel* which means "God with us." God, in his own pleasure, chose to make earth the "visited planet" by sending his dearest gift—his Son.

The biological aspect of Jesus' miraculous birth is emphasized in the Gospel of Luke, where he writes, "The Holy Ghost shall come upon thee, and the power of the Highest shall overshadow thee: therefore also that holy thing which shall be born of thee shall be called the Son of God" (1:35). For Luke, the uniquely begotten Jesus is presented in the context of a biological miracle. It was unbelievable to Joseph at first, but believable later in light of Jesus' obedient life.

In John's Gospel it is the theological significance of Jesus' miraculous birth that is stressed. The "Word" for John is God in human flesh. That the Word was made flesh has importance for all of us who have fleshly existence. From now on, human flesh will never be common. The missionary who goes in flesh to all flesh knows that Christ is there. He became one of us to help us become like him.

Other religious traditions have numerous incarnations, but none with the historical evidence that Jesus' enfleshment came. This uniqueness adds to this prestige as the foundation for missions.

(2) *Teaching ability.*—The scene was a hillside in Palestine. The quiet-spoken but easily heard young rabbi named Jesus was surrounded by five thousand seekers intently interested in his words. Before the days of microphones and amplifiers, Jesus was so skillful with his words of truth that the time for the noon meal went by unnoticed. The same one called "rabbi" (teacher) in the Gospels more than any other title, then turned a little food into more than enough for the crowd. The miracle of the five loaves and two fishes was astounding but not to be remembered as more important than his words.

There have been persons noted as great teachers throughout the history of religions. They include Buddha, Confucius, and Socrates. But none matched the miracle of Jesus' words and deeds.

(3) *Teaching content.*—Not only was the style of Jesus' teaching unmatched, so was his content. Hardly anyone can forget the story Jesus told which begins, "A certain man went down from Jerusalem to Jericho and fell among thieves...." Pithy sayings were his specialty, with such unforgettables as "Ye are the salt of the earth" and "Ye are the light of the world." There were other words of action such as "Lazarus, come forth." Volumes have been written by and about such persons as Leibnitz and Aquinas and Augustine but they are weak in comparison to those by the Master Teacher. The teachings of Jesus have stood the pragmatic test of two thousand years and remain unmatched.

(4) *Sin-free life.*—It is remarkable for such an exceptionally wise person as Socrates to live his life with only an occasional mistake. Men such as Muhammad have lived exemplary lives in the tradition of great religious prophets. Courageous persons such as Joan of Arc have performed such deeds as to be long remembered. Jesus of Nazareth, however, is without sin. He existed and exists in a category all his own because he "thought it not robbery to be equal with God: But made himself of no reputation, and took upon him the form of a servant, and was made in the likeness of men" (Phil. 2:6-7). He did all this, and did so without sin. As Paul put it, "For he hath made him to be sin for us, who knew no sin" (2 Cor. 5:21). The amazing reality behind Jesus' sinlessness was that he was not simply walking through life in a phantom fashion, but he managed grief and pain and rejection without even the hint of sin.

(5) *Identification with outcasts.*—In 1948 Mahatma Gandhi of India grabbed at his chest and cried, "Hai Rama." An assassin's bullet took his life. In this bitter irony, the man who had given India's outcastes status as "children of God" was gone from the earth.

Religious prophets in every generation have championed the cause of the poor and oppressed. Jesus of Nazareth was the greatest of such champions. From the beginning he announced his intent, "The Spirit of the Lord is upon me, because he hath anointed me to preach the gospel to the poor; he hath sent me to heal the brokenhearted, to preach deliverance to the captives, and recovering of sight to the blind, to set at liberty them that are bruised, to preach the acceptable year of the Lord" (Luke 4:18-19).

Jesus' earthly ministry was a fulfillment and amplification of that intent. While never ill at ease with the rich, famous, and powerful, Jesus took extra pains to bring release to the poor, unknown, and powerless. He became the epitomy of those who are willing to live and die for the oppressed.

Each time a drunk stumbles down an inner-city street begging for a coin for a cup of coffee, the middle-class giver knows that Christ is there. Anywhere a comfortable person crusades for fair housing for the poor, Christ is there.

(6) *Revolutionary character.*—Persons who have changed their world have been those with revolutionary characters. They have spoken and acted in a disturbing fashion to their peers and groups they targeted for change. Some have sought change through verbal and physical protest. Some have written scathing denunciations of the status quo. Others have retreated to mountain hideaways in protest of the people below.

Jesus of Nazareth exemplified revolution of the most basic type. He called for radical changes in attitude. One of his favorite phrases was, "You have heard it said, but I say unto you . . . ." Such words send chills up and down the rigid spines of those who seek to preserve the sameness they cherish. Jesus rammed the towers of yesterday but could not escape the falling stones. It finally got him killed.

Today some who identify Christ with culture, as in God being an American, seek solace in the way things are. But they look in vain to Christ for a model because he shatters those who refuse to "render unto" both this world and the ideal kingdom.

(7) *Forgiving death.*—In the mid-1840s, Joseph Smith, the Mormon prophet, was murdered by an irate mob in Illinois. That mob was partially composed of his own followers who objected to his stand on polygamy. As he was dying, he took two with him to the grave with a handgun given him by one of his friends. Members of the Church of Jesus Christ of Latter-Day Saints speak of their founder as having been "martyred."

Socrates drank a cup of hemlock and died peacefully, confident that his soul would return again to earth from a giant "soul bank."

Mahavira, the founder of Jainism, died at the ripe old age of seventy-two surrounded by his adoring monks. Muhammad died in his middle years and was buried. Legend says that Zoroaster, founder of the Parsis, died by the sword.

Jesus died forgiving. "Father, forgive them; for they know not what they do" (Luke 23:34) were his words as he died sacrificially. His death before mid-life was without bitterness or resentment but filled with compassion. This was quite a contrast from the way other world religion founders died. Forgiveness was his purpose and cry as he died.

(8) *Jesus rose again.*—Paul and other New Testament spokesmen knew that Jesus' uniqueness lay primarily in his resurrection. Peter at Pentecost phrased it thusly. "This Jesus hath God raised up, whereof we are all witnesses. Therefore being by the right hand of God exalted . . ." (Acts 2:32-33). For them, the fact that Jesus' life story did not end with the grave, compelled them to summarize the gospel in the phenomenon of the empty tomb. Paul in Athens "preached unto them Jesus and the resurrection" (Acts 17:18) which was his pattern.

The early disciples knew that Jesus' resurrection was more than a biological miracle. It was also a symbol of hope and faith. After his beautiful hymn to love, Paul argued in 1 Corinthians 15:17,20, "If Christ be not raised, your faith is vain . . . . But now is Christ risen from the dead." For all who seek assurance of life after life and eternal life in the present, that empty tomb in Israel is a sign that both death and life are conquered with meaning, joy, and hope.

Put all eight of these qualities together and Jesus stands head and shoulders above all other would-be claimants to ultimate authority in life and religion whether in a holy book or in a holy person. All other revelation is weak in comparison to Jesus. Jesus of Nazareth, in his totality, is Special Revelation of a type distinct from all others. As God in person, he stands as a reminder that only he will do as the foundation for Christian missions. Paul, the greatest theologian-missionary in church history, knew that fact in his heart and mind. Modern Pauls know the same.

That same Paul in his greatest work, the epistle to the churches in Rome, however, grants the existence of other types of revelation. He wrote, "For the invisible things of him from the creation of the world are clearly seen, being understood by the things that are made, even his eternal power and Godhead; so that they are without excuse; Because that, when they knew God, they glorified him not as God, neither were thankful; but became vain in their imaginations, and their foolish heart was darkened" (Rom. 1:20-21).

Paul argues in his introduction to the Roman letter that revelations outside of Jesus Christ lead to vanity and futility, but he does not deny that they do exist with some limited degree of validity.

To grant that God makes himself known outside of Christ does not mean the following:

1. That all religions or claims to religious truth are the same. Anyone who makes such an observation is simply not paying attention. A Muslin beating himself on the back once a year with metal-tipped thongs is not the same as speaking in tongues in a charismatic meeting. Some American Christians give in too easily to the idea that religious truth cannot be known absolutely. Christ is Truth, as he claimed.

2. That the original Buddha, Muhammad, and other religious teachers or recipients of revelation had almost as much truth as Jesus. What Jesus of Nazareth exemplified and taught is as far removed from that of other teachers as major league baseball is from kickball in the backyard. Yet, when a Christian sees the fullness of truth in Jesus and his message, he does not on that account reject anything true and holy in other religious traditions.

3. That the Bible is on an equal plane with other written revelation. As a record of God's dealings with faithful and faithless mankind, it is unmatched. This written Word tells us where we came from, how to live today, and what awaits in the future. Even more importantly, it points to Jesus. While other religious traditions have "holy books," none so clearly tell of God, man, and Jesus as reconciler between the two.

To claim that Jesus, the Christ, is the foundation for missions and all of life is to say:

1. We find our true identity as a person made in the image of God by following Jesus' model. That mythical "native in Africa" finds himself when he finds Jesus. In his relation to the Carpenter his selfhood is discovered. The unbelieving targets of mission efforts are operating only as partially human without the good news.

2. Revelation in Jesus tells us most of what we need to know about God. In human flesh we see God healing, loving, calling, urging, reprimanding, and saving. Jesus is God in the verbal tense. For us as limited seers, Jesus acts it out in terms we can see and feel. John sums it up for us, "That which was from the beginning, which we have heard, which we have seen with our eyes, which we have looked upon, and our hands have handled, of the Word of life" (1 John 1:1).

3. Jesus is the standard by which all truth is to be judged. The Bible knows little of the modern fragmentation of truths. In the inspired written record, there is little of compartments of "scientific" or "religious" truths. All missionary methods as well as scientific laboratory investigation are under the scrutiny of the One who said, "I am the ... truth" (John 14:6). Missionaries are "successful" in direct proportion to their adherence to Christ's Spirit.

4. Jesus lives today in the lives of his disciples in a way unique to him. The dominant phrase for Paul was, "Christ in you, the hope of glory" (Col. 1:27). He was describing Christ's unique ability to live in the soul of his followers. No other prophet has that ability to the degree Christ does.

5. We can be called to be God's ambassador without being called to be his judge. God's judgment of individuals and of nations is and will be one which he alone is equipped to handle. A backslidden Baptist and a Methodist "fallen from grace" act alike and smell alike on a Saturday night. Only God can handle the separation into sheep and goats of those who have never heard the gospel or hear it in a garbled fashion. Our task as missionaries is to be reporters in the courtroom of the world, not judge or even jury. This, however, does not decrease our task of announcing the good news that God and self are to be known in Jesus.

In little more than three short decades Jesus was among us. He taught and lived in such a distinct manner that to seek to outdo him is to flail against a desert sandstorm. He is the foundation of all that is. That qualifies him to be the sure and ever-present foundation of carrying out missions.

Jesus is the foundation for both mission and missions. While "mission" is God's total redemptive purpose, "missions" is the activity of the church to announce and display that purpose to all the earth. Jesus is Lord and foundation for both—and more.

Our God has revealed himself through the ages, but never so clearly as in his chosen foundation. The writer of Hebrews said it, "God, who at sundry times and in divers manners spake in time past unto the fathers by the prophets, Hath in these last days spoken unto us by his Son" (Heb. 1:1-2). That's enough to act upon in his name. That's missions!

In *Peace Child*, missionary Don Richardson tells of his discovery that the Bible must be given to any culture in terms with which they identify. He calls this "redemptive analogy—the application to local custom of spiritual truth."[2] And that's what we must do—we are duty-bound to carry the gospel of Christ to "every kindred, every tribe."

---

1. Dietrich Bonhoeffer, *Letters and Papers from Prison* (London: Fontana, 1953), p. 221.
2. (Glendale, CA: G/L Publications, 1974), p. 10.

1
The Bible:
Mirror for Missions

The doing of missions is God's favorite work. This is clear when looking into the Bible, God's mirror for missions. There is in that book a continuous and sustained account of God's revelations through a series of prophets and their inspired sayings. Along with the Christ-event, the Bible functions as the source of authority for missionary endeavor.

Scriptural authority for world missions rests not merely upon a group of isolated "proof texts" but upon the design and spirit of the Bible as it reveals God's search for persons in their communities. The Bible is God's search for man, in sharp contrast to other holy books, which are the story of man's search for God. As such, it is best interpreted thematically, with attention given to such major motifs as call, justice, grace, forgiveness, judgment, and covenant! It is not the purpose of this book to so zero in on some sections that the impression is left that piecemealing the Scriptures is a sound interpretative method. Rather, the highlighting of certain passages will hopefully serve to amplify dominant themes in the Bible.

There are some evident unifying themes of the Bible, often in spite of the fact that it consists of sixty-six books composed by more than forty authors over a period of fifteen hundred years. One of those themes is surely the spreading of God's love through missions. There are others, also, which complement that theme. As they mesh, it becomes even more apparent that even today God is reaching out through his written Word to persons able to hear, both persons doing missions and those being missionized.

The Bible, as the mirror for missions, is inspired of God. Second Timothy 3:16 states, "All scripture is given by inspiration of God, and is profitable for doctrine." The word translated "inspiration" is *theoneustos* and may mean "God-breathed." The writer wants his reader to know that God is as intimately involved in the formation and present application of Scripture as in the very act of creation itself. Thus, the Bible and missions are both dear to the heart of God.

In other words, by New Testament times it was customary to describe at least some of our modern Old Testament as utterances of the Holy Spirit of God. So by the beginning of the Christian era the term "Scripture" had come to mean a fixed body of divinely inspired writings that were fully recognized as authoritative. Jesus used that term in that sense. All his listeners knew what he meant when he said in John 10:35, "The scripture cannot be broken." Proof of this is that there was no controversy between Jesus and the Pharisees on the authority of the Hebrew Scriptures. The argument arose because they added their tradition and held it as being equal with Scripture.

For believing Christians the authority of the Bible is the authority of God himself and it is he who initiates the whole undertaking. Biblical truth is therefore not a human discovery but a divine gift. This realization helps keep the interpreter-missionary humble because he can never claim to be anything but the channel of grace and truth.

The efforts of Christian missions are rooted in the reality of history. Jesus was counted in a Roman census. The Bible is not concerned with fables and fairy tales, but with all-too-human persons who bleed when stuck and cry when hurt. Parts of the Bible would be rated "R" at your local movie house. That is encouraging in missions because people, too, are frail as dust. There is no "holy" attempt to hide the sodomy in Sodom, the lust in David's heart, or the treachery in the mind of Judas Iscariot. God called and still calls "just plain folks" to become extraordinary by attempting the unusual feat of bringing Christ to the nations. It is missionaries with feet of clay but feats of the supernatural that God still calls.

The Bible is not magical within itself. The Holy Spirit brings its words to purposeful action when applied. At that point it becomes very clear that the Bible is a divine-human book. As human, the believer can easily identify with it. As divine, it breathes the concern of a loving God. In balance the Bible also portrays God as judge. It is filled with divine authority and calls for Jesus-dominated mission and ministry. This is because, above all, it is a divine call to free faith in Jesus as Lord. Wherever Jesus is, there also is the Holy Spirit. Paul makes this clear in 1 Corinthians 12:3, "Wherefore I give you to understand, that no man speaking by the Spirit of God calleth Jesus accursed: and that no man can say that Jesus is the Lord, but by the Holy Ghost." There is an eternal contact made when the modern mission-minded reader activates the principles of the Bible. Persons inspired of the Spirit wrote as God directed. Today persons filled with the Holy Spirit become eager to do God's will in the direction of their neighbor. The Spirit is thus still at work. It is he who makes the written Word a living Word, in the jungles of Nicaragua and the asphalt jungle of New York City.

The Bible is also the mirror of modern missions because it is eternal. It speaks to every person in every culture precisely because it is the eternal, unchangeable, and transcultural Word of God. There is not a person alive who cannot relate to the call of Abraham, the struggles of Moses, and the ministry of Paul. Even better, it does not speak to persons merely on the surface but at the deeper levels.

In 1978 four persons went into retreat in a Zen monastery in Japan. They were a Zen monk, a Catholic priest, an agnostic psychiatrist, and a renowned philosopher. They emerged a few days later with their considered observations that what the human family most needs is acceptance, love, and community. The Bible speaks clearly to those universal needs in an authoritative and positive manner.

The Bible is always modern because it is a word about life from the Creator of life itself. This lends the written word a transcultural quality. The words of Genesis and Romans and the other sixty-four books speak to the human family as human. So they cut with piercing power across all ethnic groups, to all nations, and to all in spite of income or social standing.

The Bible is not only a sword cutting through cultural differences, it is a mirror or manual for missions. For the modern missionary, the

Bible contains more than adequate guidelines for doctrinal formation, worship patterns, and the maintaining of hope and faith in the
face of loneliness.

The family of man is addressed directly by the words within the
Word. On those pages persons are told they are beings of dignity,
the highest of all God's creations, made in his image. But, persons
also recognize themselves honestly as being plagued by pride,
greed, and loneliness. Man sees himself mirrored in Amos' crying
against Samaria and Jeremiah's weepings over "broken cisterns."
Wherever humans are oppressed by evil persons, the Bible demands their release. The Word of God pleads for the helpless and
the hungry and against the haughty. As long as there is a needy
person anywhere on earth, the Bible is a clarion call to action on his
behalf. Further, the Bible empowers the believers in community to
minister to those whose lives are plagued by need.

In numerous languages and at various stages, persons ask universal questions. They include: Who am I? Who is God? If there is a
God, where is he now? How can humans come into contact with
God? What happens after death? Does history have any meaning?
The Bible answers in clarity these questions. The missionary is the
point of contact to those seeking answers. Further, because Jesus is
the living Word, the Bible through the missionary provides more
than answers. It gives life because it records that all human history is
moving toward Christ. Paul affirmed this: "That in the dispensation
of the fulness of times he might gather together in one all things in
Christ, both which are in heaven, and which are on earth; even in
him" (Eph. 1:10).

The ultimate authority of the Bible is based on the foundation for
missions, Jesus. The Bible is the Word as it points to Christ and finds
its meaning and unity in Christ. Faith in the Lord of the Bible makes
this possible. Thus, every word in the Holy Scriptures are best
understood in the light of what he taught and what he did and who
he is as the living Word.

If man were a library, God would try to reach him ultimately in a
book. If he were a constitution and bylaws, God would be breaking
through to him through religious rules. Because he is a human,

God's supreme act of self-revelation was in a human, Jesus. The ultimate revelation of God is in a person. So, even the four Gospels cannot be placed on the same level as the Christ to whom they give witness. He, as Lord, is dynamic reality. It is he who both spoke and was the Word. Thus, he is qualitatively different from the Bible. As the foundation for mission, Jesus and the Bible are partners, but not equal.

As the mirror of missions, the Bible is a record in three tenses. As past tense, it is the record of the saving acts of God in history. It is a testimony of the power of God among chosen peoples of the past. In the present, the Bible gives guidance to mission efforts. As future, the Bible lets the missionary know he is on the winning side. It is the lordship of Christ to which all efforts are moving. Thus, this greatest of holy books gives meaning to all that is—past, present, and future. It is in that manner that the Bible is the source as well as the result of inspiration.

It is in the Bible, as in the Christ-event, that the divine and human are blended perfectly. In inspiration and in modern missions, God uses men—not machines. The Bible writers were men of weakness, prejudice, and passion as we are now. Although led clearly by the Holy Spirit, each one brought to the biblical writing task his own peculiarities. Some were well-educated and others were definitely not men of letters. Modern missionaries range from the PhD. leading a discussion of Christ among Hindu scientists to the carpenter building latrines in Honduras. The Bible writers were men allowed to look at God and his creation each in his own way.

The dominant example of the writer's own ways are the four Gospels. Matthew was a lawyer and very interested in "tricky" legal questions brought to Jesus by the Pharisees. He was also careful to document the validity of Jesus' acts by citing Old Testament parallels wherever possible, almost as if preparing a docket for a court appearance. Mark wrote in much briefer strokes. He has been called the "Jack Webb" of the Gospel writers because he gave "just the facts." Luke was a physician and very aware of human need. Women and children are spotlighted in his Gospel with regularity. Luke's Gospel is also one of joy and singing. Angels break out in song. The Holy Spirit is central in presenting Jesus' life as Luke points out as well in Acts. John paints a portrait, not a photograph of Jesus. John is concerned that Jesus come across to his intellectual Greek readers as an expositor of great truths. The beautiful but realistic picture one receives of Jesus through the writers' combined efforts is an accurate and inspiring one. Nothing at all is detracted from the biblical witness by noting the varying personalities. Rather, from the four Gospels combined is a fuller one because of their different perspectives. So it is with current missions effort. The nurse aids the doctor who has learned from the seminary professor who aids the media specialist who interacts with the church growth specialist. The result is a work for and through Christ which is as wide as it is deep. In each case, biblical inspiration and missionary effort, it is the cause of Christ which profits.

The more than forty writers did not have their natural senses dulled or their faculties suspended in the inspiration process. They functioned as fully human while controlled by the divine. So it is with missions-minded persons today. We function best when controlled by the Spirit, but never do we become less than human in the process.

There is no line to be drawn between the divine and the human. We cannot say of any part of the Bible or of missionary service, "This is divine" or "This is human." Both areas are as sunlight through a painted window. The sunlight is not in any way diminished by the window. Rather, it is made suitable for the room. God speaks no special heavenly language. He comes to us in language we can understand through human instruments. So it is with missions. We go out as human instruments with a divine message. So it was and is with Christ, the Bible, and with missionaries.

It is foolish to ignore either the godly light or the human instrument in ancient or modern revelation. To ignore either is to shortchange the marvelous miracle that God works when he meshes the true to bring us to truth and light. In God's plan, both he and his followers are essential. The same is true when that plan is worked out in missions.

As a mirror for missions, it is imperative to bear in mind that the

Bible basically deals with broad principles and not narrow precepts. It is we who are trusted, in a gigantic risk by God, to apply those basic principles to specific situations. That is where the process of mission strategy and application begins and continues. To note that Abraham was called almost four millenia ago does no good unless we can discern what God would have us do four minutes from now.

Sometimes the Bible's commands are of universal application. For example, "Thou shalt not steal." Sometimes they refer only to the specific instance before the writer, as in Paul's letter to the Corinthians and his rulings on marriage. The Bible assumes that its readers will be sensible people. Its writers express themselves quite openly, taking no pains to so guard and qualify their statements. Nowhere do they warn us that the truths they write are to be weighed against statements one may read elsewhere. It is up to the reader to apply common sense as it is when he applies the Bible's truths to his missionary or ethical situation.

As Bible inspiration and interpretation is done in the context of the efforts of others, so is mission effort. One cannot simply read a "daily chapter" in the Bible without giving some attention to who wrote it, when it was written, and to whom. A missionary who does not assess his situation in a cultural context may commit the same type of fragmenting error. He has to remember with whom he is dealing.

In 1979 a famous evangelist in America went to central Nigeria to conduct an evangelistic crusade. Upon his arrival at the hotel lobby where his party was staying, he noticed a monkey in a cage. The monkey grabbed at his suit coat as the evangelist walked by as if to get his wallet. That night in his opening illustration before a packed soccer stadium, the evangelist said that he had not come to get the people's money as a man's wife or monkey might do. Immediately the stadium was racked by loud booing and hissing. Objects were thrown at him. The interpreter tried to explain but to no avail. The next night's sermon started out with the evangelist trying to explain his previous mistake. Again the people grew restless. The crusade had to be cancelled. In that part of central Nigeria one never refers to a human being as a monkey. In fact, the most insulting curse one can put on another is to compare him with a monkey. The context was not considered. The crusade was cancelled.

To understand a culture one must know the context. The task for Bible application is the same. Paul was hurt when he wrote the Corinthian correspondence and angry when he addressed the Galatians. He was in a gentler mood when writing the Colossians. That change of mood makes a difference. No missionary would address an angry mob in the same manner as a friendly audience. The Bible demands no less respect than an audience. It deserves serious common sense and devotional approach.

Devotional Bible study involves letting your imagination roam freely. Think of the situation. Put yourself in the place of the actors. Get into the mind of each participant. Mix that attitude with one of prayer. Let your soul linger in the presence of God. Then get off your knees and on your feet. The task of world missions is too urgent to dally in extended meditation over truths already observed. Failure to bow before Bible study is as tragic as failing to do after knowing. As a mirror for missions, the Bible is to be seen, heard, and acted upon. As a devotional guide, *The Foundation for Missions* is designed to lead to action, not mere sentimental warmth in the heart. With that in mind, let us proceed to examine the themes within the Bible lending themselves to missionary application.

A major missionary motif in the Bible is that of God as Creator of all that is. As created beings, all humans everywhere find their true identity only in relation to God.

From the beginning the creation accounts in Genesis are universal. The message is clear: one God created one world and one human family for the purpose of being one But, sin (rebellion) against that oneness became a factor and the result was separation. This has a message for the modern missionary. We are in the business of reconciliation. The goal is the oneness of the human family finding itself in the one God. So, missions by necessity crosses over the artificial barriers put up by man in his attempt to hide from God. The missionary comes with the good news that the God who seeks his own is a good and loving God who wants only man's fulfillment. The missionary is the indispensable link in that communication circuit.

In the creation account in Genesis we learn something of God's nature as power and love. God loves man. That is the central message in missions. We see that mirrored early in the first book of the Bible when God bends over to breathe life into Adam (Gen. 2:7). God's love was so rich and risky that he entrusted all this earth to us. When we messed things up by not wanting to operate in submission to him, God still wills us back to him in love. This is a strong warning against any attempt to coerce, trick, or delude any person into coming back to God.

According to the creation account, God originally provided Adam with everything he wanted (vv. 8-14). This paradise was topped off with a loving companion who perfectly complemented him (v. 18). God still desires that kind of life for us. The mission task is to make that desire clear to all of us, even when we tend strongly not to believe something almost too good to be true.

A second major missionary motif is that God still calls specific individuals to be leaders of groups in a specific and special manner. Abraham, Albert Schweitzer, and Annie Armstrong are specific examples of God's specificity in this purpose. God so loves the world that he calls. That theme is an apparent one when the Bible is read with an overview. Moses, Gideon, Ruth, David, and Amos are but a few of those persons given responsibility for whole groups of others. The nature of the call varies from blinding lights to burning bushes to speaking donkeys, but the purpose is the same: to name a person and so empower him that he can draw a people back to their loving God.

Such called persons become the focal point of God's dealing with his people. There could have been no Exodus without a Joshua, no early missionary enterprise without Paul and his peers, and no church without disciples. That is the way God has chosen to redeem; that is to say, through humans leading humans.

An example was Moses, a man of missionary mold. He was

called, authorized, and went (Ex. 3:1-10). There was little hesitation when he finally understood that the same God who called him would empower him.

A third major theme in the Bible as a mirror for missions is that of God's universal interest in all peoples. Jesus urged his disciples to make other disciples in all the world. Modern missionaries are discovering with men of old that there is no aspect of human life or tribe of people anywhere in the world in which God is not interested. Oh, there was and always is the temptation to limit God's love because of obvious physical differences, but the Bible will not allow such blindness. Jonah in the belly of a great fish and the good Samaritan bandaging wounds become two of many symbols of God's universal love. There is no limit to the gospel marked by age, income, or skin color. God's universal love transcends all those artificial fences.

A fourth major theme in the Bible as mirror for missions is prophetic courage. Today the popular definition of a prophet is one who sees mysteriously into the future. This idea originated among the peoples with whom the Hebrews came into contact in the Old Testament era. They had the idea that some kind of foreign power overtook a seer for a brief period which allowed him to go beyond space and time. They were seen as "out of their mind" while communicating truth to their listeners.

Today the popular mind thinks in terms of a possession or a trance into which the medium goes—a la Edgar Cayce and Jeanne Dixon. But such a view is narrow and misleading. Biblical prophets are best understood to be "forth-tellers" rather than a "foreteller." The prophets then are understood as men who received from God the truths which they spoke in his name—in the present tense. Often they are seen as entering into the prophetic calling through "hearing the word of God" and commissioned to speak that love in integrity. This inspiration was the process by which the truth came to him by the Holy Spirit. While he saw God's word to him as distinct from his own thoughts (Jer. 14), it came with such a power that he knew instinctively that it was from God (Amos 3:8).

The prophets of the BC era were "overwhelmed" spiritually but not physically. A prophet was compelled to speak "the Word of the Lord" in spite of natural fears that might have been used as an excuse. The "Word" could come by a vision (Isa. 6:1 ff.), or suggested by some figure in everyday life (Jer. 32:8), or by a highly unusual event (v. 8).

With courage unique to their vocation, the prophet's primary purpose was to preach to their contemporaries. They cut through hypocrisy as they spoke to God's children who were guilty of political, social, and religious abuses. True prophets, as a rule, had messages of warning to deliver (Jer. 28:8-9). Anyone who cried, "Peace, Peace," was immediately under suspicion as being inspired by something other than the Lord. True prophets cried out for righteousness. It took courage. It took looking into the eyes of their peers and calling for cessation of comfort when necessary. Cheaters and blasphemers were condemned, no matter how hard they cried or complained that they were true followers of God. No less courage is required by the modern speaker and struggler for righteousness. In the midst of such struggle, Amos, Hosea, and Micah stand beckoning from the past on the Bible's pages saying that it can be done; that is, the Word can spring to life.

Social insight for the former prophets and the current missionaries is universally applicable based on the biblical theme of righteousness. This concept cuts across cultural lines because it is a call for meeting the demands of a group of relationships. Each of these relationships brings a whole network of obligations with it. When those obligations are met, righteousness is fulfilled. Modern missionaries bring their zeal for God into the fray wherever there are relationships not being fulfilled. So, missions become broader than demand for conversion to God. Even the casual reader of the Bible cannot ignore the thematic demand for social justice.

Wherever Christian missionaries go, they leave in their wake persons who exhibit mercy. The new converts are those who show forth their salvation by caring for the poor, the fatherless, and the widows (Prov. 29:7). The new fellowship of the righteous, called the church, is marked by its giving spirit (Ps. 37:21). Further, the new believers live at peace with their neighbors (Job 31:1-12). The products of righteous missionary effort are also those who take care of their family needs. In return, God grants them peace because they give peace to those around them.

Today, those who are righteous are those who have responded in faith to God's act in Christ and therefore have given substantial respect to those about them. This carries with it the necessity of admitting that one does not have the capacity within him to keep a kind of covenant relationship. Only Christ can supply such power. That is part of the good news; Christ saves and gives power to change all lives around the saved. This reliance on God Paul calls "faith." For Paul, faith in God alone can produce righteousness and provide power for improving relationships. Also, God puts his stamp of approval on the believer who exercises faith. God himself approves of us precisely because we respond to his love through our faith. True restoration of relationships comes from reliance on God alone. Therefore, for Paul, to be considered righteous by God is because we quit depending on our own ability to achieve harmonious relationship to God and his creation (Rom. 5:1).

In a vital sense for Paul, personal salvation and social righteousness are closely linked. The modern missionary who separates them in any fashion is not true to God or his written Word (Rom. 3:24; 2 Thess. 2:10 ff.). So, to be a part of salvation (reconciliation between man and God) is to become a part of righteousness (peacemaking in the human family). That makes missions the business of bringing peace wherever there is strife. The two elements of God's love, personal and social, can never be separated. Man must rely on God for both.

Social action called for in the Bible does not lessen the believing ambassador's necessity for evangelism. The Bible makes it clear that "evangelist" was a title, not of an office, but of an activity of first-century Christian missionaries. In fact, the title is hardly ever used outside of Christian literature. In fact, in the New Testament, the office of evangelist was not clearly distinguished from that of evangelists (Gal. 1:8). In other words, then and now, one sent forth in Christ's name is to proclaim the good news of God in Christ. He is to "placard" or display that good news by reconciling man to man and man to God.

Missions consists of doing both social action and evangelism. There is no division between the two. Anyone interested in the welfare of human beings in God's name will seek to bring both sacred and secular peace. Then "soul-winning" will continue to stress the necessity of conversion and growth toward individual and social wholeness. The Bible knows nothing of a partial ministry toward a person or group of persons. To choose the soul or mind or spirit or body and ignore the emotion or will is not to minister in a biblical manner. As "Jesus increased in wisdom and stature, and in favour with God and man" (Luke 2:52), so must the missionary minister to persons in wholeness.

Social action and ministry may also be seen as "cultivation evangelism": ministry in the political or rehabilitation arena may provide opportunities to enhance verbal witness later. As Paul puts it in 1 Corinthians 3:6-8, "I have planted, Apollos watered; but God gave the increase. So then neither is he that planted any thing, neither he that watereth; but God giveth the increase. Now he that planteth and he that watereth are one." It is God who uses the combined efforts of evangelists, physicians, teachers, and agriculturalists in the combined task of missions.

Adding all these themes together makes it clear that doing missions is doing God's favorite work. After all, missions began in the heart of God. The whole arena of missions is the scene for God's struggle to bring his most precious creation back to him. He made us to find ourself in him and he yearns for the close of history when those responding to him in faith will dwell with him. He desires this so much that he spared no price to provide us with the opportunity to find our way back to him. To make that trek back possible, he calls missionaries to point the way. From Abraham on, he has beckoned for a leader of many to follow. These leaders have responded in spite of hesitancy and fear of failure. They have become great trailblazers back to God in direct proportion to their faith in God. While leading whole clans or nations, these missionaries have discovered that God wants to gather others along the way, even those not specifically slated to be a "light to the nations." The pilgrim people are called to pick up hitchhikers as they journey with no restrictions as to how they look or what they earn, God's universal love is for all and any who will respond in faith. Occasionally God calls courageous prophets to call persons to repentance. They speak to their people about the hypocrisy of trying to honor God while keeping others away from him. These prophets run the risky business of "speaking the truth in love" (Eph. 4:15) amidst people who have no ears to hear. But, prophetic modern missionaries continue in that tradition because they have heard the call of universal love from the God who is love. Inevitably spiritual concern for righteousness and reconciliation bring about evangelism. Proclamation built on service is biblical. Often Jesus healed before or while he spoke to the crowds.

The fact that God still calls unworthy and weak followers is a sign that he is still concerned with missions, his favorite work. God knows that the church is the only hospital in town where the patients are part of the staff, but he calls for healing anyway and waits for that staff.

ADDENDUM
Paraphrase of Exodus 3:1-14

"God's Call to Moses"

There was once a fellow named Moses who was a produce manager in his father-in-law's grocery store. He had worked there a long time without much advancement. Nothing much exciting ever happened around the neighborhood.

One day Moses was helping to unload a produce truck at the back of the store when he felt a breeze on the back of his neck and a strange and mysterious presence.

Moses looked at an incinerator where they burned cardboard boxes. The fire was getting hotter and hotter and more of the boxes were being burned up.

Moses immediately said, "I'm going back inside the store and tend to my own business where such strange things don't happen.

I'll be a lot safer in there. No, wait a minute, I guess I'd better see why these boxes aren't being burned up."

Then Moses realized that God must be behind this whole happening. At that moment God spoke to him out of the incinerator and said, "Moses!" Moses was scared but he still said, "Yes, I'm the one."

And God said, "Take off your apron and shoes and socks and come over here closer. Anyplace can be holy ground when I make it so, even out behind your father-in-law's grocery store."

God kept on talking, "I am the God who led Abraham and Jacob and Lottie Moon and a lot of other faithful followers." Moses grew frightened and hid his face behind the truck, trying not to look back at the incinerator.

A few minutes later, though, Moses listened again as God said, "Moses, I have not forgotten my people who are now being held in bondage in the Soviet Union. I know that they are not allowed to worship freely or evangelize like they want to. But now I am ready to turn them loose on the world so their faith can be an inspiration to all who would follow me. I am going to set them free from that Communist nation and bring them out to a land where they will be free both spiritually and physically. They have suffered long enough. I want you to get ready to go over there to set them free."

Then Moses, peering from behind the produce truck, said, "Surely there's been some kind of mistake here. I'm just a poor produce manager who turned down a chance last year to be a Sunday School teacher."

God replied, "Get ready to go, Moses. All you need to know right now is that I will go with you. You can help me get those people out of that land where they can't worship me in freedom and lead them here where they can."

Moses said, "All right, I'll consider it but I've got in a whole batch of new tomatoes that could ruin while I'm gone. The first thing they're going to want to know is by what authority I've come to set them free. What can I say then?"

God smiled and said, "You just tell them that the only God that is, is on your side."

2
Creation and Call

By all current standards of potential performance, Mrs. Parker should have been retired years before I met her. She was a seventy-one-year-old widow when she was my first-grade teacher. Oh, yes, she was also the teacher of thirty-one other pupils in that one-room schoolhouse in rural east Texas. She had to cover a lot of subjects in the four grades she taught. This she did very well. For example, she taught the sound of the letter "B" by filling an old long-necked milk bottle with water. As she poured out the water, we all heard the "B, B, B" sound.

Mrs. Parker was unaware that one should not pray in school. We not only prayed twice, but we were required to memorize Scripture. Often she would ask the class for our individual favorite verse. The favorites were "God is love" (1 John 4:8) and "Jesus wept" (John 11:35) for some reason. Then Mrs. Parker would recite her favorite verse, "In the beginning God created . . . " (Gen. 1:1).

This lovely lady had a tremendous impact on my life. It was she who led me to Christ at age seven. A revival was being held at the Baptist church across the street from the school. She turned out school and we all went to church for a morning service. As the invitational hymn was sung, I got Mrs. Parker's permission first, and went forward to announce to the pastor that I wanted Jesus in my heart.

In spite of my profound respect for Mrs. Parker, I confronted her one day with the fact that she had been holding out on the class. Genesis 1:1, I had discovered, was longer than the five words she had been reciting to us. When I told her, she patted me on the head and said, "I know, but those five words are the foundation of our faith because in them we know who made us and we see his power." I never forgot those words.

Moses Maimonides, a Jewish scholar of the medieval era, said it more eloquently, "The foundation of foundations and pillar of all wisdom is to know that the First Being is, and that He giveth existence to everything that exists!"

Genesis 1:1 can be seen to be the most striking passage in the whole Old Testament. The concepts contained therein are still a challenge to the modern scientific mind. Yet, there is no need to see Genesis as in conflict with modern scientific theories. Genesis was never intended to be read at a gathering of natural scientists. The Genesis account is designed to remind us that it is God who made us, and we are his. The writer speaks from faith to those who read under the guidance of the Holy Spirit. The truths imparted in that process are beyond the capacity of the natural sciences to interpret. The scientists can seek to discern and recreate the technical processes by which creation occurred, but their efforts are as futile as analyzing baseball by deciding the shape and weight of a baseball bat. The discoveries of science and theology supplement rather than contradict one another. Without the piercing objectivity of science, theology can become only superstition. Without theology, science can be an instrument of moral evil.

Another "problem" in the mind of some moderns is the one created by the existence of some creation accounts in other cultures which roughly parallel the creation accounts. In various ways other ancient peoples affirmed that the world emerged out of a chaos. For example, the Babylonians claimed that the universe's structure is a result of a bitter struggle between the god of order and the goddess of chaos.

The Genesis account, on the other hand, is not reliant on such a struggle. There was therefore no insistence on a ritual repeating regularly that early struggle. For the faithing Hebrews, creation is a direct result of God's power. This represents a central difference. The Hebrew was able to assert God's unity and power even in the context of their neighbors who saw creation in terms of many gods struggling. They were freed from a nature religion which seemed to make it necessary to bow before elements of creation. For the Hebrews, God was the only one worthy of worship.

The modern missionary is constantly involved in the same process. He has to assert God's power and love in the midst of cultures where persons tend to worship almost anything except the one true God. The modern American may not worship the Thunderbird at the top of a totem pole, but is likely to worship the one at the new car showroom. The Ashanti peoples of West Africa may seem to make a god out of the yarn. It is their way of trying to get to their chief god. The missionary in either context must proclaim the truth of the one God who can be known directly in Christ.

The missionary message of the Genesis account is that creation is the starting point of history. The same God who will draw all human events to a close by having all bow at the feet of Jesus is the one God who started the whole process. The missionary simply stands in the middle of that process, proclaiming both the beginning and the end because of meaning he has found in the middle. He is part of the church which continues the tradition of being the chosen people of God.

In Hebrew and Christian theology, then, creation and current events are directly related. Creation is simply the first of God's saving acts. He creates to have fellowship, the same fellowship he still desires (Ps. 74:12-17).

The writers of the Genesis account are also very eager to convey that there is a harmony and inherent goodness in God's creation. When God speaks anything or any being into existence, it is for the purpose of assigning it a specific task. Even the heavenly bodies are created to give glory to God (Gen. 1:14-19). At any moment he could allow the world to fall back into chaos. The psalmist wrote of this in Psalm 104:29-30, "Thou takest away their breath, they die, and return to their dust. Thou sendest forth thy spirit, they are created: and thou renewest the face of the earth."

Part of the message of missions is that God as Creator has not completed his task. Every baby born is his product. Any order, social or scientific, has its origin in God alone. This is especially important in a world prone to give credence to science or artificial gods. The call to missions is a call to exemplify one's submission to his Creator on a continuing basis.

The missionary determines his priorities on another message in the Genesis account. That message is that the jewel of God's creation is man himself. The earth is even primarily present to be our dwelling place. The prophet Isaiah stated it thusly, "God himself that formed the earth and made it; he hath established it, he created it not in vain, he formed it to be inhabited" (45:18). Therefore, the missionary is sent to the crown of creation. He is not wasting his time with anything less than the best.

Man is presented as made in God's image (Gen. 1:26-27). As made in God's image, man is to relate back to his Creator. He is to be God's representative on earth. He is to function as the administrator of God's works. Similarly in Psalm 8 the idea that man is just a little lower than the angels is quickly followed by the thought that God has put all things under him. Man, as able to respond, is held responsible before God for all other created beings. It is in that context that any called person goes forth as missionary. He is God's representative with the accompanying power and authority to get the job done. The job is to bring all persons to the realization that the God who made them is the one who wants to recreate them in faith.

The New Testament makes it clear that Christ had a central place in creation. Hebrews 1:2 says, "Hath in these last days spoken unto us by his Son, whom he hath appointed heir of all things, by whom also he made the worlds." That concept is made even clearer in Colossians 1:15-17, "Who is the image of the invisible God, the first-born of every creature: For by him were all things created, that are in heaven, and that are in earth, visible and invisible, whether they be thrones, or dominions, or principalities, or powers: all things were created by him, and for him: And he is before all things, and by him all things consist."

The modern ambassador for Christ, therefore, is not bringing a nice little commentary on how to have a better life. He is representing the Redeemer and Creator as well as Savior and Lord. The message becomes, "He who made you loved you enough to die for you." The message of history is that, from beginning to end and at all the places in between, life is under the purpose of God as revealed in Jesus of Nazareth. John's Gospel begins by echoing the beginning of the Genesis account, "In the beginning . . . ." The tie-in is undeniable from the Bible's perspective. The one who redeems us is the one who made us. There is no need for idols or images or lesser gods.

Genesis 1:1 should be properly translated, "In beginning God . . . ." There is no *the* beginning with God. He has always been. That is one of the major motifs of the gospel message. The one true God whom we represent is not in need of any other gods. He is not dependent on time or space or any other being for his existence. That message is especially important in cultures where there are multiple gods. The God of the Bible has no room for other would-be claimants to his throne. While men reach out to him through other religions, he seeks to bring all his creation back to him.

The word for "created" in Genesis 1:1 is unique to the one true God. This term is never applied to anyone except God. Only God can *bara* (Hebrew for "create"). This verb is never used to mean being reliant on any kind of materials. God creates directly without any need for any other substance. He is not reliant on any *thing* or any other *god* for his creative powers.

Genesis 1:3-5 contains insight into the missionary message as well. "Created light" is the reflection of the eternal light of God's own person. There are numerous nature worshipers who bow before the sunrise or a sunset or the stars of the heavens. Today about forty million Americans will read their horoscopes in the daily newspaper and about five million will read their Bible. That is indicative of the fact that even "modern" nations cannot discern between the light and the Light of the world. Genesis 1:16 says, "He made the stars also." This phrase comes almost as an afterthought to the statement that God made the sun and the moon. What God can make "with the flick of his wrist" some persons are ignorant enough to bow before and call "god." It is a modern as well as an ancient problem.

Genesis 2:7 states that man "became a living being." The original

Hebrew says, "a living *nephesh.*" For the Old Testament writers, man does not *have* a soul, he *is* a soul. The soul is the total person. Any missionary strategy that divides persons on any basis is one which does those persons no lasting service and one which also does not do justice to the biblical record.

Genesis 1:26 states, "Let us make man in our image, after our likeness: and let them have dominion over the fish of the sea, and over the fowl of the air, and over the cattle, and over all the earth, and over every creeping thing that creepeth upon the earth."

To be "in God's image" holds tremendous responsibility for all of us. As God freely creates, we have the obligation of making that creation better or worse on a daily basis. We are of a different sort than the animals. The animals live by a lower instinct but we are created for a higher purpose. The animals are to procreate but we are to bear children for more reasons than just the fact of bearing them. The animals simply adjust or perish in the environment they cannot change. We can change that environment for better or worse. That is the challenge of being human.

The central difference between man and other created beings is a distinction not made by those religions native to India. It is estimated that today one third of the food supply in Calcutta will be consumed by rats. Jains allow rats to roam freely in their monasteries, spreading disease and consuming much of the food supply. Traditional Hindus venerate the Brahma cow while allowing "untouchables" to go hungry. They elevate the tiger, the elephant, and the monkey (among other animals) as beings in which a man's Atman (soul) may have previously existed and to which it may return. The Christian missionary proclaims that the gospel is for humans. Cows do not hold prayer meetings and horses do not witness. Without apology and based on the biblical witness, Christians assert that we as humans are the beings on the earth who matter most, but this is precisely because we are responsible for the maintenance of the rest of creation. That maintenance is the human privilege and challenge. It is not just for humanity's benefit.

Because humans have misunderstood the word translated "subdue" in Genesis 1:28, they have mistreated God's planet earth.

Humans have thought that "subdue" meant that nature existed solely for our benefit. So, we have, especially in the twentieth century, squandered the earth's resources. When the U.S. alone consumes one sixth of the earth's natural resources used by the nations of the earth annually, this is cause for reexamination of our entire value system.

Missionaries in some cultures have concluded that their witness would be clearer if their life-styles reflected a concern for nature rather than the consumerist mentality of the American people. These effective missionaries have lived in mud huts among the people, eaten their food, and mixed that style with love. Too often foreign missionaries have mixed their gospel message with an affluent life-style. The "natives" could not hear the message of love because of the flashy daily life of those preaching sacrifice. The "compound mentality" of the missionaries has hurt. This is the attitude that the missionary is to live in a beautiful house on the hill behind locked gates. He makes an occasional jaunt into the native culture on Sundays for worship or "to do mission work." This is the opposite of allowing the nature and native-oriented life-style to speak volumes about the human concern central to the gospel.

The creation materials in Genesis thus contain at least four truths applicable to modern missionary effort. They are:

1. God is without equal as Creator and Redeemer. He is dependent on nothing or anyone for any of his activities. There is no room for other gods.

2. Man is the highest of all creation. He is barely below the angels and infinitely above the animals. As existing in God's image, man is more responsible for what happens on the planet earth than any other creature.

3. There is a God-desired and ordained order and beauty to the universe. Men and other beings are created to fill a certain spot in the universe. That order is restored through Christ.

4. Human beings, as the target of missionary effort, are never to be viewed as partial beings. They are not to be seen as souls to be saved but humans to be redeemed.

The second central motif in the first book of the Bible is that of the call of God. In Genesis 1—11, the reader finds the human family painted in broad strokes. The scene shifts in chapter 12 from mankind to the man Abraham. From this point forward the chosen people are at center stage.

Genesis 12:1-3 reads as follows, "Now the Lord had said unto Abram, Get thee out of thy country, and from thy kindred, and from thy father's house, unto a land that I will shew thee: And I will make of thee a great nation, and I will bless thee, and make thy name great; and thou shalt be a blessing: And I will bless them that bless thee, and curse him that curseth thee: and in thee shall all families of the earth be blessed."

This section is pivotal to an adequate understanding of God's plan for the peoples of the earth. Abraham was God's way of getting to the whole world. This call of Abraham marks the beginning of the method by which God has been dealing with the human race ever since, about four millenia.

There are four major missionary lessons to be learned from these three brief verses:

1. God elects specific persons and peoples (v. 1).

There is always something arbitrary about God's choice of an individual. To choose one inherently means not to choose a number of others. The Genesis writer does not bother to explain why Abraham was chosen above the rest. God, in his wisdom, chose Abraham as the best man available at the moment. It is apparent as Abraham's story proceeds that Abraham was far from perfect morally. The Bible, as in the case of David, and Noah, makes no attempt to hide each one's moral failings. For example, in Genesis 12:10-20, we read that Abraham practiced deceit with Pharaoh, trying to persuade him that Sarai was his sister, not his wife. Even the pagan Pharaoh turned out to be more ethically straight than Abraham and reprimanded him for his lying.

What Abraham had going for him was faith and it is for that that he is best remembered. He never understood God's nature completely but he faithed out his life with confidence. That made him usable as an instrument of God's peace to his nation and to other nations. Abraham was chosen for his potential usefulness, not for any innate talents. The same principle applies to the chosen today. The elect are no better than others; they are simply selected for service.

Today there is an unhealthy romance of missions. The missionary is often pampered, partied, and exhibited as if he were a freak of nature. His level of commitment is honored and his sacrifice held as semi-sacred. The result is an unhealthy stigma often placed on returned missionaries who "couldn't cut it" on the foreign fields. Home missionaries are not honored as often or as much because they have not gone as far geographically as the foreign missionaries. All of this romanticism and artificial veneration overlooks the biblical emphasis that God calls people to do a job, not bask in the glory of adoration from a large audience. The elect are no better than others, they are simply selected to do a job.

2. God's choice's for a blessing (v. 2).

Here we see that the chosen are blessed. Abraham received a sevenfold blessing:

(1) He would father a great nation.

(2) God would bless him in his own lifetime. The blessings which were about to come his way would not have to wait until future generations.

(3) Abraham himself would be a world figure; his name would be called great on a worldwide basis.

(4) He would be a blessing to others. Abraham's worldwide fame would therefore be for all the right reasons, as a blessing. He would be famous, not infamous. Abraham now knew he would be blessed by God for the purpose of helping others. His high office should inspire responsibility, not merely the sheer joy of special privilege.

(5) Abraham's blessings could and would be shared by those who received him. This was because they were receiving God through receiving his servant.

(6) Anyone who sought to discredit Abraham would in that act reveal their own insensitivity to God who was at work in Abraham. Therefore they would invite God's wrath upon themselves by despising God's emissary.

(7) Abraham's good influence on the world was to be worldwide.

Here we see an early biblical indication that God has universal designs on the faith of the human family.

These seven blessings promised Abraham are a godly combination of the temporal and eternal. The temporal included promises of protection, guidance, and material blessings. The chief blessings Abraham could anticipate, though, were the spiritual ones. The main spiritual benefit was the privilege of an intimate fellowship with God. Abraham was to be escorted with honors into the throne room of God. There he would even be told in advance the future plans of God. Missionaries around the world can testify that there are no geographical limits to access to God. God hears prayers from Angola as well as from Alabama. When he chooses one to do his will, he lets him know, sometimes gradually, his perfect will. The key today, as it was in Abraham's day, is still faith on the part of the elected missionary. The limits of blessings are never due to God's stinginess.

God did not choose Abraham and his followers as pampered pets called to receive blessings implicitly denied to others. Rather, people of faith are to be pipelines of blessing. They receive special blessings only to channel those blessings on to others.

Genesis 12:4-9 pictures the faithful Abraham in Canaan, a land strange to him but one in which he is at ease because that is where God wants him to be. Modern missionaries know that downtown Chicago or the bush in Togo can be comfortable if that is where God wants them to be.

Abraham, however, was crippled in his intent to show allegiance to God by the faithlessness of his nephew and companion, Lot. Many a missionary has had to display faith in spite of a retarded child, an unwilling wife, or a faithless set of parents. That set of circumstances, however, can be the occasion for strengthening both the faith of the missionary and his clan. The faithful one who functions in spite of unfaithful family members has temporary tension but with the potential of being a light to the neighborhood in spite of that tension.

In verse 7, we see that Abraham built an altar. He was able to see God even when surrounded by Canaanites. This was, after all, the land which God was to give Abraham eventually. Abraham stands as an inspiration to the modern missionary of faith who looks to God when surrounded by enemies who are potential recipients of God's mercy. Abraham, like human servants today, did not know God's ultimate will for him in advance. He found that will as he followed his Lord in faith.

The section Genesis 12:10—13:1 portrays Abraham, the man of faith, during a brief sojourn in Egypt. Here we see the capacity of Abraham for deception. He passed off his seventy-five-year-old wife as his sister. The Genesis writer here does not comment on Abraham's lack of morality but merely reports it. Abraham is portrayed as a man unprepared for this threat of a foreign and hostile culture. He was not the first ambassador for God so threatened by the situation that he turned to ungodly methods. Invariably, those threatened people bring dishonor to their God and to themselves.

In Abraham's case, the pharaoh's pagan morals turned out to be higher than his. It must have been embarrassing for the father of the great Hebrew nation to be deported from Egypt by a pagan pharaoh. Abraham's God was dishonored by an unfaithful steward. But, later Abraham was able to recover and be remembered as a champion of faith. It was thus because of God's faithfulness to the covenant and Abraham's growing faith that he could be a blessing. God is always able to rescue and preserve his will beyond all human failure. This story of Abraham's initial failure is a reminder that anyone to whom a godly promise is given is often the greatest enemy of that promise. The determining factor is the missionary's faith or lack of it. God never changes.

Genesis 14 presents Abraham as a world citizen, confident of taking God's blessing to all peoples. His historic meeting with the mysterious Melchizedek is filled with opportunity and challenge. In this instance Abraham bows in the presence of one who worships the same god he does. There is no bitterness, only humility, as these two spiritual giants exchange kindnesses. Many an ambassador for Christ has discovered to his surprise that there are believers all over the world who are merely waiting to be told who it is they believe in. Paul preached the same truth in Athens, "Whom therefore you ignorantly worship, him declare I unto you" (Acts 17:23). The missionary can never go to a place where God has not already been, if only in a veiled fashion.

Genesis 18 is the account of the destruction of Sodom and Gomorrah in spite of the pleadings of Abraham. This section is especially graphic in communicating the truth that sometimes the will of God is thwarted even when both God and his missionary are faithful. The gospel must still be heard to be effective. In spite of God's loving initiative and his faithful's zeal, some are still bound not to believe.

In verse 1, we find an elderly Abraham waiting for a visit from the Lord. When the messengers appeared, Abraham makes him welcome even in the midst of the day, very unusual for a desert dweller. He spared no energy or resource in making them welcome. He had waited long for their arrival. There were no circumstances dire enough to make him unresponsive to the Lord.

Too often the modern missionary prays for a visit from the Lord and is too busy or preoccupied to recognize him when he comes. That may be due to the fact that sometimes God does not come in the form we expect him to. He may come in the form of a hungry orphan instead of a responsive potential convert to Christ.

In verses 9-15, Sarah is pictured as a semi-willing but doubting hostess. She laughed to herself when she heard one of the messengers announce that she and Abraham would soon bear a child. She knew that she was so old that her menstrual cycle was meaningless. The immediate retort to her weak faith was, "Is anything too difficult for God?" Here again we see faithful Abraham surrounded by family members who just cannot believe that God can do anything, even those things impossible to human flesh alone.

Verses 17-19 represent God talking to himself just before the impending destruction of Sodom and Gomorrah. Abraham is about to learn that the greatest blessing a faithful follower can find on earth is a knowledge of the nature and purpose of God. That knowledge in this instance is that there is a limit to God's patience in the face of unfaithfulness. In God's will, righteousness must stand. In this monologue, God is pictured as deciding to tell Abraham what he is about to do and why he is doing it. That way, when Abraham knows of God's strong desire for righteousness, he can warn future generations.

In verses 22-33, Abraham is allowed a high human privilege, that of asking God what he is intending to do. Note that Abraham never forgets who he is addressing. In an attitude of prayer, he begs God to spare the cities but does not push beyond his authority to do so. Abraham was willing to leave the final decision to God.

Genesis 22 paints another beautiful portrait of the faithful Abraham when called upon to sacrifice Isaac. Isaac was not only Abraham's long-awaited and beloved son, he represented the very covenant between God and Abraham. If Isaac perished, there would be no physical sign of the Lord's presence and blessing on future generations. If Abraham surrendered Isaac to God, there would be nothing tangible left. What God had promised and finally given, he now seems to want to take away. The faithful Abraham was once again not expected to fully understand, merely to obey. That is the essence of faith. That was Abraham. That is why the two are remembered as synonymous. This was a test to strengthen Abraham's faith. He stood the test in spite of the fact that he was being asked to give up his future. Long before Jesus was to utter the phrase, Abraham was learning to "Take therefore no thought for the morrow" (Matt. 6:34).

In Genesis 22:8, Abraham assures his precious Isaac that "God will provide." There is no indication here that Abraham anticipated a way out of the demands upon him and Isaac. He was simply speaking the words of trust that God would act in faithfulness to his nature and covenant with Abraham. God did provide a substitute, but not until Abraham's faith was tested and found true.

Even today God asks his ambassadors to be totally faithful. That often includes the willingness to give up family and/or the certainty of the future. Many a young missionary couple have stood before a commissioning service crowd uncertain of the support of their parents. Their future was to be marked by strange sights and sounds and scrapes, but they were willing to risk because they knew that to follow God's call was to follow a call marked by love and power.

Their cost was faith and the reward a peace in knowing that they as blessed could be a blessing.

The two clear missionary themes of Genesis are creation and call. Adam and Abraham share with us a common reminder that in being human instruments of his good news, we share in faith the responsibility of turning the world right side up again.

ADDENDUM
A Paraphrase of Genesis 1:1-13

Before there was ever anything at all except him, God made the earth and all things in innumerable galaxies.

The breath of God moved across a giant nothingness and turned it into something with shape and organization.

Then he spoke, "Right now let there be light." And with the intensity of the energy required to light a million football fields, there was light!

Then God saw the light and pronounced it good. It was so good that he separated it from the darkness.

God then gave that bright light the name "Day" and the darkness he called "Night." That division made the first full day.

Then God's almighty voice was heard again. "Right now I want a separation in all those waters; so that some water will be divided from the rest." Suddenly there was a division between the sky and the waters left on earth.

Then God gave a new name to those waters above. He called that place "Heaven" and it became a symbol of hope and beauty. All this separation took place on the second day.

Then God's booming voice was heard again over the face of the whole planet earth. "I want all the waters of earth gathered into one place so that they are divided from the earth." Without a moment's hesitation, it was so.

Then God called all that dry land "Earth" and the gathered

waters he called "Oceans." God backed off and took a good look and said, "I like that!"

Then God said, "Let all that dry land produce beautiful greenery." And it was so in great abundance and beauty. God said again, "Now, that's very good!" And that happened on the third day...

3
Champions of Challenge

The case study method of teaching popularized in the 1970s has revolutionized the classroom. Instead of the lecture or sermon model, some churches are using case studies as a way of communicating truths and methods of Christian living and serving others as missionaries.

A case study is an account of something that could or did happen. It is a "slice of life" from which lessons can be learned. Teachers can use case studies to develop skill in seeing critical issues and in analyzing the motives of the parties involved in the story told. Basically, it is a method designed to bridge the gap between theory and practice.

There are many types of case studies, including an unfinished story or "complete the cartoon caption." Usually the case study is followed by a series of suggested questions for group discussion. Reactions to such case studies may vary greatly. Some groups may want to brainstorm certain parallel answers to a dilemma. Some members may want to debate possible answers to the dilemma presented.

The case studies in this chapter focus on fine Old Testament men long remembered for the faithfulness to God in spite of horrible circumstances. You may want to share this chapter with a mission study group of some kind. These case studies are presented, no matter what type of response you choose, for the purpose of raising questions relating to the mission of God in the world and our part in it.

Case Study Number 1: Moses

Please allow me to introduce myself before I ask for some advice. My name is Moses. I am best remembered as the leader of the He-

brew tribes in the Exodus from Egypt and during our consolidation period just prior to their entrance into Canaan.

The only source of information for my life and work is found in the Bible, especially in the book called Exodus. I am introduced in Exodus 2 as a baby. Due to the clever intercession of my sister and mother, I am rescued and given shelter as a powerless infant. I was raised in the Egyptian court as a highly favored adopted son until the day I slew an especially evil Egyptian taskmaster. I was forced to flee Egypt and I ended up in the land of Midian. There I found employment as a shepherd and married the daughter of my employer.

In Exodus 3 is found my call from Yahweh to go back to Egypt and bring a people out who were and would be special to Yahweh. I did not volunteer to be the liberator of Israel. I was not even especially known for my piety. I sort of stumbled into history when I stumbled onto a holy place in the course of my duties as a shepherd. In short, I was drafted for the job.

(Stop here.) Think about or discuss these questions:

1. What kind of person was Moses prior to his call in terms of faith?

2. What qualities had Moses already shown that would make him an effective ambassador later?

3. What are some parts of Moses' personality that God would have removed to make him a faithful spokesman?

4. How important is it to know who sent an emissary when he comes on an errand?

5. Did God have his hand on Moses already before his call? How can you see God leading you up to this moment?

What changed me was that call. The burning bush became a symbol for me. I was about to burn myself out for God and yet not become consumed. From that day onward, I have been a man set apart by God's selection. But it was more than election. That day God empowered me for a specific task in a particular moment of *time. There was no doubt about what God wanted. When he was willing to give me his name, then I knew that he wanted me for a task dear to him.*

I soon discovered that the call to follow God is not an invitation to sit around and analyze the call. Other generations could do that later but I had to get with God's program. The scene shifted from Sinai to Egypt. Then the hard part started. I had to get both the Egyptians and the Hebrews to believe what God had told me on that mountain. Fire on the mountain soon turned to the smoky haze of doubt. I was to mold a new community of God's believers out of a bunch of motley people who doubted me and God at every turn. It was going to be a difficult thing to do but God had an idea. He molded the people together (I helped a little) through a common experience.

God gave me special powers on the spot to help get that bunch of Hebrews together. The pharaoh and I engaged in a seesaw battle of signs and plagues. The only reason I won, we both knew, was because Yahweh was so much stronger than the pitiful Egyptian gods. I was no wonder-worker or wizard.

When the last plague came, the Lord had helped me get the people ready to go. We were saved from a terrible slaughter of the firstborn of every kind. That miracle is to be long remembered. Our oldest male children were saved because God has a special job for us. We remember that night as the "Passover."

(Stop here.) Think about or discuss these questions.

1. What is the most dangerous assignment God has given you in the past year?

2. Do we necessarily measure missionary commitment by geography or danger or misery?

3. What political forces in our world make it difficult to be a follower of God?

4. To what degree does God put us "on the spot" when he gives us special gifts?

5. Has God called you to a specific task and then "uncalled" you after it was completed?

As soon as we got out of Egypt, our faith was tested again. The Egyptians were chasing us with superior weapons and intentions of getting us back to be their slaves. Then, at a critical moment, God alone stepped in to save us. I learned that day that sometimes God cannot share his power with us, not even those he has especially called to be his prophets. All I could do was stand and point, "Fear ye not, stand still, and see the salvation of the Lord, which he will shew to you today" (Ex. 14:13). God alone was able to deliver his people.

That part was glorious. To see those waters parted for our safe crossing and then to see those vicious taskmasters killed was more than my soul could stand. But, I needed that vivid memory because then we had forty years—count them—forty years of wandering! There we had the basic struggle of survival, all the time that "a land flowing with milk and honey" was waiting on us. There was the matter of a daily diet which God soon took care of, with manna. Our enemies were everywhere it seemed. We knew the general direction of Canaan but seemed to keep losing our way and being detoured. If we did not learn anything else during that time, we at least learned the lesson of daily dependence on God alone. I kept reminding the people that if our God could part the sea, he could surely send us an oasis in the desert.

At once the highest and lowest moments of our whole wilderness stay was the receiving of the Law at Mount Sinai. It was a low moment because the foolish and unfaithful people chose that moment to build a brazen idol. I guess God knew it was time to give some irreplaceable rules to live by. The revelation on that mount confirmed and climaxed the deliverance from Egypt. I knew then, and the people began to see, that God wants a relationship with us that is intensely personal and he demands allegiance in every area of life. We found God to be a "zealous" one who would have no time for other gods.

I am an old man now. I have seen and learned a lot in my years. My eyes are a bit moist now and my heart is saddened. I know I will never get to go with my people to Canaan. I sinned against God and that was even when I knew the rules. For awhile I was the *obedient mediator between God and his people. I will go down in the records of my people as proof that there is no perfectly obedient man in all of Israel. Only God is finally just and we are just directly in proportion to our dependence on him.*

(Stop here.) Think about or discuss these questions.

1. How are you like Moses?
2. What are the "wildernesses" for modern missionaries?
3. Which of the Ten Commandments are most essential to keep in missions activity?
4. Does God call people who are perfect to serve him?
5. What role does patience play for the faithful emissary of Christ today?

Case Study Number 2: Hosea

One day a man named Hosea found this letter in his mailbox. What should he do?

But, first, before we read the letter, it would help us understand the situation better if we knew this about the man Hosea.

Hosea was the only one of the writing prophets in the Old Testament who made his home in the northern kingdom of Israel. He lived in the eighth century BC and was a younger contemporary of Amos. Hosea's main purpose in life was to call the Israelis to repentance from the growing corruption of morals, religion, and politics which marred their day. Early in his life Hosea married a woman named Gomer who would prove to be a faithless wife. He made numerous fruitless efforts to reclaim her. After she bore him three children which they gave sad but symbolic names, she left him for other lovers. But, Hosea was so forgiving that he went to the slave block and bought her back for a very dear price. Again and again he tried to win her back to a life of purity and love.

Then one day Hosea realized that what Gomer was doing to him, Israel was doing to God. Israel's unfaithfulness was breaking God's heart. Israel was dancing off after strange gods while God wanted them to return. God was willing to forgive if only Israel would cease her adulterous and idolatrous ways.

The Israelites' adulterous ways were as corrupt as those of Gomer. They were going up to the old Canaanite shrines and trying to mix Yahweh worship with paganism. They tried to honor Yahweh with the grossest of sexual immorality as a part of their worship. Hosea was heartbroken. One day he found this letter.

DEAR HUSBAND:

Thank you for all you have done. You have taken me when I was nothing but a temple prostitute. With you I have found respect and honor in the community. Our three children are wonderful and you have been a caring and patient father with them. They love you very much.

I hope you will understand when I tell you that I just can't take it any more. It is no reflection on you as a man, but my old ways are calling me back. Just the other day I saw a man I used to know at the old sacred groves of Baal. I wanted to run away with him then but decided to put things in order here first.

Please try to understand. I don't know if I'll ever be back but right now I don't see how. Kiss the kids for me and tell them that their mother loves them very much.

Please don't come after me. You wouldn't want me here if I didn't want to be here. In my own strange but unfaithful way I'll always love you.

                                                    Love,
                                                    Gomer.

(Stop here.) Think about or discuss these questions.

1. How is Gomer in the letter like all of us?
2. How is God like Hosea in the book of Hosea and in the letter?
3. What would you have felt if you were Hosea?
4. What good qualities did Gomer have, if any?
5. Is it ever right to mix the worship of anything else with the love of God?
6. Would you have paid a dear price to get Gomer back? Why?
7. How big a factor is love in the current doing of Christian missions? Why?

8. What difference would it have made to Hosea if he had lived after the time of Jesus? How is love different to you since you met Jesus?

Case Study Number 3: Amos

How would each of these four persons be likely to react to the book of Amos?

1. Father Daniel Hammons:
   Catholic priest; never married; missionary to Libya; teaches school; politically liberal; comes from an affluent family; grew up in the Detroit suburb of Grosse Point; attended parochial schools; fifty years of age; goes to daily mass.
2. Mr. Tom Grayson:
   Thirty-two years old; has PhD. in history; teaches at a junior college; has two grade-school children; does volunteer work for civic club; teaches Sunday School in a Methodist church; grew up in poverty.
3. Cindy Marsten:
   Seventeen years old; senior in high school; smokes pot occasionally; wants to go to college next year; major undecided; has her own new sports car; not required to clean her own room; has had an abortion; occasional church attender in Protestant tradition; about to become engaged to a bread truck driver.
4. Mrs. Margaret Cox:
   Seventy-one years old; widow with two sons and six grandchildren; grew up in middle-class family in Canada; lives on a farm; sponsors "candystripers" at a nearby hospital; votes Republican regularly; member of a Lutheran church but infrequent attender.
Here is Amos' story:

Amos was called to be a prophet without any previous preparation. He was not particularly religious in his youth partly because he was too busy trying to earn a living as a part-time sheepherder and a part-time fig gatherer. Amos was a poor boy who grew to deeply resent the wide gap between the income of the poor and that of the rich in nearby Jerusalem. Amos was a country boy from Tecoa. His virtues were simple and honest. His eyes were sharpened by the austere life of the desert and his nostrils from the stench of the Dead Sea. Some people called his home area the Valley of Doom. His simple faith was strengthened because he grew up near nature. His God was the one who made the clear sky and fresh water.

When Amos was thrust from rural Judah to urban Israel, the change was a drastic one. His senses were offended by the stench of the crowded marketplaces and his eyes seered by the sight of the dancing girls. His moral sense was offended by the sale of poor people for the mere amusement of the rich. Amos could not stay quiet.

His irate attitude broke into poetry. At first his eloquence was a surprise even to Amos. His convictions were so deep that his soul soared to the heights of beautiful but pathos-filled thoughts. Amos was a keen observer of life. For him, a holy God could only be served through a pure and holy life. Amos was filled with the insight that can only come through the eyes of an outsider. The people of Israel were so calloused by their own life-style that they could not see their vast sinfulness. He had eyes to see where others were blind. Maybe that is why Amos often thought to himself that God puts a person in a different place to proclaim his message. Amos could easily see the dishonesty of the courts, the mistreatment of the poor, and the moral sicknesses within Israel's upper classes.

Amos was most offended by the silence of the professional prophets and he strongly denied that he was any part of them. He refused to let his name be associated in any way with the prophetic memoirs. They were blind in Amos' eyes. They gave in to social pressures and spoke soft words rather than harsh warnings.

Amos was marked by the genius of his style. He made great use of the repetitive refrain. But his style did not interfere with his theology. For Amos, the coming judgment of God was relentless and unavoidable. His primary demand was that of repentance before it was too late. The heart of Amos's simple theology was the deep conviction that only a nation with daily social fairness and compassion can find real favor with God. As the proclaimer of simple truths calling for simple honesty, Amos laid the groundwork for the champions of challenge to come after him.

Amos' originality comes out when he openly attacks the worship patterns of his day. For Amos, ceremonial worship has no value. God is only interested in justice. Worship without justice makes God sick.

An example of Amos' judging poetry is as follows: "Hear this word, you cows of Bashan, who are in the mountain of Samaria, who oppress the poor, who crush the needy, who say to their husbands, 'Bring, that we may drink!' The Lord God has sworn by his holiness that, behold, the days are coming upon you, when they shall take you away with hooks, even the last of you with fishhooks" (Amos 4:1-2, RSV).

(Stop here.) Answer each of these questions as if you were one of the four persons described above and if you were yourself.

1. What do you find most oppressing about your own society?

2. If God wrote a front-page editorial in the New York Times today, what would he likely say?

3. How is Amos like a missionary you know personally? How unlike?

4. Do evangelism and social ministry go together in missions? Why?

5. Can a rich church ignore the needs of its community and please God by giving large amounts of money to foreign missions?

Case Study Number 4: Jeremiah

The model used here is that of "Problem-Solving." Here is the problem.

Hello, my name is Jeremiah. If you go to church or synagogue much, I imagine you have heard of me at one time or another. Sometimes I am called the "Weeping Prophet."

I was active from 626-580 BC. I like to think that I was a sensitive man, responsive to life as I saw it around me. Nature especially spoke to me and I loved to draw parallels from the almond blossom in the spring (1:11-12); the hot air of the desert sirocco (4:11); the times of the swallow, turtledove, and crane (8:7); the drives of the young camel and wild donkeys (2:23-24); and even in the pathos of the heavens (2:12).

I was never what you might call a socially adjusted man. Throughout my life I was set apart from the other believers. I was never accepted by my countrymen. The priests and prophets ridiculed and persecuted me constantly. My own family resented and disowned me (12:6). I was denied the joy and comfort of a wife and family (16:1-2). Most of the time I even felt separated from God (17:17).

Yet, all the time I was helped along by an awareness of God's call and presence (1:8). My security came to be not in acceptance by my hearers but in the power of the godly word I was called to speak (1:9).

Many images could be used to describe the role I played for God. In the Bible I am called a prophet to the nations (1:5); an intercessor for the people (11:14); a harvestor in the vineyard; a refiner (6:27 f.); a speaker of parables and a parable himself (13:1-11); and a fortified city (1:18).

I was born in the village of Anathoth, just two miles northeast of Jerusalem. My father was a priest named Hilkiah of the favored tribe of Benjamin. I was affected by Hosea whom I heard prophesying once.

My call to be a prophet came in 626 BC when I was still in my teen years. At first, like our hero Moses, I was reluctant to serve. But, the power of the divine word came over me (1:9).

Four major concerns were reflected in my sayings to the people:

1. The corruption of true religion;
2. The lure of the nature cults;

3. Judah's spiritual insensitivity to the will of the Lord; and

4. The impending invasion of a foe from the north.

I was especially upset because I remembered our people's early devotion to God. That made it hurt so badly to have to remind our people that we had exchanged our one true God for other gods. This was made worse because we were led to do that by our priests, prophets, and political rulers. My people were even engaging openly in the raucous fertility rites of the foreign cults (2:20).

So, naturally, I issued urgent plea after plea for our people to return to the God who desires nothing but the best for his people. When I opened my mouth, it was evident that Hosea had influenced me. I spoke of adultery against the eternal covenant God wanted us to keep.

I was pleased to see the reforms brought to our people by Josiah and during this glorious period I was relatively quiet. A prophet is never happier than when he can keep his mouth shut! But, then Josiah died and my people reverted back to idolatry under Jehoiakim. As soon as he took office, I went straight to the Temple and warned that our refuge should not be in official religion. My address caused a great uproar among the people. They rose up and threatened to kill me. I barely escaped with my life. During Jehoiakim's reign, time and time again I begged my countrymen to obey God (22:1 f.), but they would not.

When Carchemish fell to Nebuchadnezzar in 605 BC, I was greatly affected. I was kept from going near the Temple area. My friend, Baruch, and I went into hiding. Once I did come out of hiding to go to Tophet to prophesy there, but that move proved to be a mistake. Pashur, the priest there, when he heard my words, put me in stocks and left me overnight. He expected that to silence me, but the next day the Lord led me to deliver the worst saying yet against Pashur (19:14 f.).

I guess I am remembered as the "weeping prophet" because I was unafraid to reveal my deep inner thoughts. There has never been a prophet who did not wonder at times whether he was doing the right thing. I grieved out loud that I was born a man of strife (15:10) and had drawn hostility (15:17). I confessed openly that fol-

lowing God had caused me isolation (15:17). Once I even accused God of tricking me (20:7). The careful reader will note that in midst of these cases; however, God overcame my egocentricity by his strong presence and word (15:19 f.).

Zedekiah was the next king God called me to prophesy to. He lacked force and stability of character even though he was not as openly wicked as Jehoiakim. My main task during his reign was speaking against the many popular false prophets who told the people everything was fine. I publicly lamented the ungodliness of both prophet and priest (23:9 f.).

The big moment under Zedekiah came for me in 594 BC when there was a gathering of foreign powers in Jerusalem to plan co-operative effort against Babylon. I placed thongs and yoke bars on my neck and addressed the leaders with a word from the Lord. The message was simple: the one true God will dispose of nations as he sees fit because he is the power and Creator of the whole earth. So, they must subject themselves to his rule (27:1 f.).

I spent the last years of my life in Egypt. There the Lord gave me the last prophecy I ever received, called the prophecy of the new covenant:

"Behold, the days come, saith the Lord, that I will make a new covenant with the house of Israel, and with the house of Judah: not according to the covenant that I made with their fathers in the day that I took them by the hand to bring them out of the land of Egypt; which my covenant they broke, although I was an husband unto them, saith the Lord: But this shall be the covenant that I will make with the house of Israel; after those days, saith the Lord, I will put my law in their inward parts, and write it in their hearts; and will be their God, and they shall be my people (31:31-33).

(Stop here.) Use these five steps in solving the problem: Should Jeremiah have agreed to be a prophet for God?

1. Define the problem.
2. Gather the data by reviewing the records, including your own feelings and opinions.

3. Fit the facts together and determine how one fact relates to the whole. For example, why would Jeremiah have seen the necessity for God's having a new covenant with his people?

4. Determine possible solutions. For example: Jeremiah could have been a priest, joined the king's court, and been a popular prophet, fled to Egypt earlier, or kept his mouth shut.

5. Determine the best solutions.

6. Take action!

Case Study Number 5: Isaiah

How would each of these three persons be likely to react to Isaiah's testimony?

1. Dr. Jack Toland:

Medical doctor; operates bush medical clinic in East Africa; father of three children; forty-nine years old; politically conservative; grew up in poor rural family; reads Bible daily.

2. Dr. John Tarpson:

Twenty-nine years old; medical doctor; affluent; has lake cottage and new foreign sports car; big tither at church; active deacon; home falling apart; has no time for wife and family; seeing a friend who is a psychiatrist.

3. Mr. Wayne Dorsey:

Thirty-three years old; operates grocery store; three children; surrendered for foreign missions service at age fifteen but never pursued possibility; has college degree and one year of seminary; occasional church attender; wife never attends.

Testimony:

My name is Isaiah and it means "the Lord is salvation." I prophesied in Judah and Jerusalem during the days of Uzziah (783-742 BC), Jotham (742-735 BC), Ahaz (735-715 BC), and Hezekiah (715-687 BC). Thus, I shared the prophetic stage with three giants: Amos, Hosea, and Micah.

My father was Amoz. I was born in 760 BC in Jerusalem. I was called as a teenager. I married a prophetess. She bore me two sons which we named "a remnant shall return" and "the spoil speeds, the prey hastens."

My prophesies spanned a whole generation of forty years. I withdrew from public life about 725 BC and gathered a group of disciples about me for their instruction. It is they who collected and preserved my prophetic messages. These messages reveal new understandings of holiness, sin, judgment, repentance, forgiveness, and faith. I came to see holiness as a picture of my own sinfulness. I saw sin as a reliance on religious ritual rather than on God's power and love. This led me to see and proclaim that God is directing all of history in readiness of having his perfect pull on earth.

All of this led to my central emphasis on faith. Some say this made the latter ministry of Jesus Christ easier. I saw that a nation can survive only with resolute faith in God alone (Isa. 7:14). This led me to be one of the first Hebrew prophets to proclaim the coming of a personal Messiah. This coming, I proclaimed, would surely lead to a paradise on earth.

All of these insightful teachings were based on God's clear call to me to be a prophet. When discouraged, I fell back on that moment many times for strength. Here's the way I remember it.

It was the year our beloved King Uzziah died. We were all fearful that the loss of such a leader would bring our nation to disunity. He had ruled Judah for forty years. The Lord came to me as a king seated on a throne. I knew instantly that it is on him only that I should be depending. For a brief moment I was privileged to look into the very throne room of God. There I saw a heavenly council convened to look into the future of his people. Suddenly I knew that I was to play some kind of central role in our future as a nation. But I felt so unworthy and I dwelled among a people so unworthy of God's special attention. I feared I would fail in whatever task he would give me because I am so weak when compared with the strength of the one true God. I cried out, "Woe is me! I am weak!"

At that moment God cleansed me and set me aside for his chosen task. I was cleansed and forgiven and ready to attempt any-

thing. The burning coal made me a new man. I would never forget what forgiveness through faith could do. I volunteered to be sent out even before I knew what I was called to do. "Here am I! Send me!" I cried. I was simply making myself available. The call was clear. I was to prophesy until Israel changed.

(Stop here.) React to Isaiah's testimony as if you are one of three described above. Add yourself. Answer these questions:

1. How can a believer know he is called to a task?
2. What kinds of tasks does God call his children to do today?
3. Does a believer have to spend his life in misery if he is not faithful to God's first call?
4. Does one have to have a lifetime call to be effective for the moment in missions?

The case study is an effective teaching method because it gets us involved. That is a lot like missions. The Bible is a mirror of missions because we see ourself struggling to be faithful among a group of people who need the light and love we bring.

ADDENDUM
Paraphrase of Amos 6:1-7

Woe to you who live in luxurious comfort in Nashville and Birmingham, and to those who feel unafraid in your new summer homes and recreational vehicles.

You who think you are blessed especially merely because you have so much material wealth.

If you think you are something, go down to Miami Beach and fly out to Beverly Hills where houses sell for $3 million. You never win in the rat race for more money. Someone always has more than you.

You who live only for the moment will be made to pay one day.

You can pay me now or pay me later. What I demand is giving mercy to the poor and oppressed.

Woe to you who carry Gucci purses and have an alligator symbol on your shirts and sweaters.

You stretch yourselves out on king-size water beds and watch soap operas all day, filling your heads with fantasy.

You eat only the best prime veal and grow fatter by the month while the poor folks across the tracks go hungry.

You buy the best of 8-track tapes and listen to songs about serving me but you spend more on the tapes than you give to orphans.

You drink alcohol by the case and spend $80 an ounce for the finest perfumes but you don't care a bit about the 3,500 who will starve to death in the time it takes you to dress for a carnival ball.

So, when my judgment comes, you will be the first led out to destruction while the poor laugh at your foolishness.

4
Isolation or Involvement?

Newsmagazines were not found on stands at the corner of Olive and 12th in Jerusalem during the times of Jonah, Ezra, and Nehemiah. If they had been, they would have told the story of these three men of God in a style native to the area and understood by the weekly reader. Certain pages would have contained advertisements, others editorials, others special features, and even others would have featured personal interest stories. The last half of this chapter is written in the style of such a newsmagazine, the *Israeli Item,* but first a little background information.

The little book called "Jonah" is unique among the current collection called the Minor Prophets. It is placed among the prophetic books in spite of the fact that it contains no prophecies. Its style is that of a historian, even though it is not placed among such history books as 1 and 2 Kings and 1 and 2 Chronicles.

That placement is probably because the book is definitely more than a biographic sketch of the historical prophet briefly mentioned in 2 Kings 14:25. It is usually assumed that the book was written by the eighth-century prophet whose name it bears. But, twentieth-century biblical scholarship has insisted on a later date for its writing. This is primarily because of the universal theme of the book. In time-sequence, the book reflects very closely the second part of Isaiah, with emphasis on the missionary spirit of Israel.

It is also accepted by most modern scholars that Jonah did not write the book. It was about him and not by him. The tenses in the Hebrew make it clear that the author was looking back past the events. Further, the author has to go to great pains to describe the former glory of Nineveh, which had fallen in 607 BC. Today it is generally agreed that the book was written in the period immediately following the reforms of Ezra and Nehemiah, or about three centuries after the fact of Jonah's ministry.

The theme of the book of Jonah is that of God's universal love, even to those seen by his chief ambassadors as pagan heathen savages. It is presented in opposition to the Judaism near the time of Jesus which displayed suspicion toward Gentile neighbors. In Jonah we see a forelining of the verse appearing in 1 John 4:7, "For love is of God; and every one that loveth is born of God, and knoweth God." It is a rebuke to any people so narrow and bigoted that they try to decide for God what peoples he will redeem. This little book exposes the Jews' narrow nationalism and shows the universal redemptive design of God for all the human family. It was an attempt to awaken the national conscience concerning their international neighbors.

The teachings of Jonah are directly applicable to the modern missionary methods and message:

1. God is personal and vitally concerned with the welfare of all peoples.

2. God demands righteousness among his chosen people and all others.

3. Salvation, covenant, and being on mission are all directly and innately connected.

4. The missionary must constantly reexamine to determine whether his values are in tune with God's.

The separate books today known as Ezra and Nehemiah were probably originally one book called Ezra. The book of Ezra as we know it today relates the history of the Jewish people from their return under Zerubbabel from Babylon to their own country in 536 BC to the arrival of a second body of exiles under Ezra in 458 BC. It is our best source for historical detail in the period it covers.

The book we know today as Nehemiah is separated from Ezra by a period of only thirteen years. The record is comprised of Nehemiah's visit to Jerusalem in 445 BC, his repair of the city walls, and his measures to assure the proper keeping of the law. The Nehemiah we meet is a model for those who would serve as a model missionary in many respects, including:

1. A balanced combination of self-assurance and humility in trusting God.

2. Energetic activity mixed with persistent prayer.

3. Mixing faith with practicality. Such balances are still much needed in contemporary mission effort.

Now let us turn to the pages of the *Israeli Item*.

On the inside cover we find "Letters to the Editor." Among them we read:

DEAR SIRS:

You guys are unbelievable. Here we are in the midst of getting some new walls around Jerusalem and you are still writing editorials on the beauties of Babylon. I say let's get these walls up before bad weather hits. Why worry about how things used to be? That makes as much sense as trying to relive yesterday. If God wants us here now, why worry about how it could have been? Let's get on with the work.

Signed: Impatient

And we see another:

DEAR EDITORS:

Doesn't anyone around here care about whales anymore? I'm starting a new group called "Save the Whales." Why, just the other day I heard about a guy who crawled around inside one of these most beautiful of God's creatures to spend three days and nights. Who cares about Nineveh? I wish I could find the guy who caused that whale so much pain. The nerve of that guy! I mean, unless we care about whales, who will? They can't defend themselves. It would have served him right if the whale had just kept him down there. See you at the rally.

Signed: Fred

Page 2 carries a couple of clever ads among the classifieds:

Help Wanted: Only Jews need apply. Eight to 5 work on new city wall. Must have at least one year's experience as manual laborer. Also needed: some guards to keep away foreigners. Must be unafraid to kill those heathen if necessary. Call 666-1112.

Godly Marriage Mating:

Have you been wondering who your Jewish daughter will marry? There are so many dangerous possibilities around nowadays. Since we're in Babylon, some not favored of God have overrun everything. Now they want our daughters. Avoid such tragedy. We have more than 2,000 Jewish boys on file in our computer bank. Call any day except sabbaths.

That section is followed by an explanation of why Ezra has been chosen "Man of the Year" for 458 BC, and therefore is the "cover story" for this issue. The editor writes:

We have been criticized for our choice of a religious person as "Man of the Year." We are prepared to defend that choice because a religious faith, as many of us remember from Babylon and Persia, is the only sure foundation for any nation. It was Ezra who reminded us all of last year of the importance of faith in the one true God. That faith is important, he showed us, in a time when courage is demanded but tending to weaken. He modeled for us such courage when he went to Artaxerxes Longimanus and got our freedom for us. Ezra walked unafraid among world leaders because he knew that God was on his side.

Secondly, the man Ezra was unafraid to tell us that we need some moral fibre. This brilliant man knew it was futile to talk about rebuilding walls and the Temple unless we are willing to be rebuilt from within. He has studied architecture and engineering enough to know that any building is just as good as its foundation. It was Ezra who reminded us of the necessity of keeping ourselves pure from heathen women while at the same time seeing them worthy of God's love.

Thirdly, Ezra knew the importance of building a nation around the vitally important practice of worship. We had been neglecting Temple services. Even when we went occasionally to worship, we brought God second and third best offerings. Ezra shamed us into realizing that in work and worship, second best is never all right with God.

Fourthly, Ezra reminded us that we are never better than our leaders. We had let almost anyone serve as a temple priest and immoral men were trying to point us to God. Ezra's pure moral example helped us to see how far off the other priests were. What a missionary of morality was Ezra in 458 BC. May God give us more like him.

Finally, Ezra brought us more than judgmental bad news. In fact, he will be best remembered here for the good news that God holds bright promises for those faithful to him. Maybe we saw that a little clearer because Ezra pointed out that divine judgment befalls those who fail to keep morally straight.

Thank you, Ezra, may next year's Man of the Year be as good as you!

Pages 5 and 6 carry an interview between Barbara Walkers and Jonah, entitled, "Jonah Returns in Triumph." It begins with Ms. Walkers asking the question:

BW: Well, Jonah, you're quite a celebrity all up and down the coast of Israel. Are you about to recover from your ordeal?

Jonah; Yes, it was really something. I knew I could do it all along. There was never a doubt in my mind that God could redeem a city even as wicked as Nineveh. The people there are not Jews, you know. Oh, by the way, I'd like to say hello to my parents. They are living in Central where my dad is still a true and successful prophet.

BW: (I'm sorry, we can't put that in print.) Now, Jonah, about all this confidence you seem to have. That's not the way it was, according to some reliable informants to the *Israeli Item.* We hear that you were pretty frightened and resentful at first. Isn't that true?

Jonah; Yes, I'd never been appointed a missionary before. In fact, I'd never been out of the territory before. I didn't know what to do when the call came. At first I thought God had the wrong fellow.

BW: So, what did you do then? I mean, when you heard that God wanted you to go to Nineveh, I guess you fell on your knees and asked forgiveness and got yourself prayed up. Is that what you did?

Jonah; No, to tell the truth, I ran as fast as I could away from God. If he didn't have any more judgment than to call a country bumpkin to preach against sin in sinsick Nineveh, I wasn't at all sure that I wanted to serve him, especially so far away from home.

BW: Our sources tell us that you left home. I find that a bit strange since you now say you were running away to keep from having to leave home.

Jonah; Yes, I never thought of it until just now, but you do have a point. I've learned a lot of things in the past few weeks. One of these things is that the alternative to serving God is often worse than simply doing what he wants in the first place, no matter how frightening the challenge is. But, I didn't want to go to Nineveh. They're not Jews, you know.

BW: That's the second time you've said that in the past five minutes. Of course, everyone knows that the Ninevites are not Jews. What difference does that make?

Jonah; Well, I grew up the son of a priest. Everything was "kosher" this and "Jewish" that and "pure" the other. My father drilled into me the spiritual superiority of the Jewish people because we've been chosen to witness by our purity. I was left with the impression that pure religion was something that the faithful believer does not do. Then, God came along and wanted me to do something, and with foreigners. That was just too much at once. But, now I know that was wrong. We're no better than others. We're just a peculiar people with a job to do by doing, not by failing to do a long list of things.

BW: Tell us about the boat and the big fish.

Jonah: Need I remind you, Ms. Walkers, that I am definitely Jewish. We're a pastoral people. We feel most comfortable when around sheep and cattle. Anyway, I was so eager to get away from God's presence, I decided to go to Tarshish. That's the most faraway place I'd ever heard of. I figured God was a local god who wouldn't be in a place so far away. Surely our Jewish God didn't go off the coast.

BW: Don't do theology, Jonah, just give us the facts.

Jonah: Oh, OK, but I've learned so much about God lately that I can't help but preach a little. I got to preach a lot in Nineveh, you know.

BW: The facts, Jonah!

Jonah: OK, where was I? Oh, yes. Well, I got to the coast, bought a ticket for the "Tarshish Tulip" a medium-sized boat with what I later was to discover was a wild crew. The captain was named Marsuk and had a short temper. At first he didn't want me on board but when he saw my money, he let me get on and we were off.

BW: Wait a minute, now Jonah, you ran away to keep from having to deal with pagan foreigners. Now you pay money to be surrounded by a whole crew of them.

Jonah: Barbara, you have a way of seeing irony. Maybe you ought to be on television whenever it's invented. Yes, there I was, doing just what I told God I wouldn't do. I learned right there on that boat that the only thing worse than risking doing of God's will is missing it. It actually would have been much easier to go ahead and go to Nineveh in the first place. Since I got back last week, two people have come by to tell me similar stories of how they tried to run away from God but couldn't. Nineveh was not nearly as bad as the hold of that boat. It didn't smell like the "Tarshish Tulip" that day.

BW: Then what happened?

Jonah: I was so exhausted from running I went to sleep in spite of the stench. I have no idea how long I slept.

It seemed like only a few minutes when I was awakened by an angry sailor. As I opened my eyes, I realized it was the captain. Boy, was he mad! He demanded that I pray. You know, even the ungodly are sometimes more faithful to their dumb idols than we are to the one true God. Do you believe in God, Barbara? I hope you don't mind if I call you Barbara.

BW: No, that's all right. But, I do mind if you continue to preach. This is a magazine, not a pulpit. And, besides, it makes no difference whether I believe in God. Now, go on with your lousy story.

Jonah: It makes all the difference in this great world whether you believe in God and which god you believe in, Barbara. That's what the crew and I learned that day on that boat. All the prayers to the lesser gods made no difference at all. It was only when we all turned to the true God that something happened. I'm not the first missionary who ever learned that.

BW: What did happen?

Jonah: They made me confess God and the fact that I was a chosen man among a chosen people. Before I knew it, I was proclaiming God as the God of the sea. My mouth was amazing even me. It was as if God had control of my tongue. I was saying, "I fear the Lord" and I really did, even when I did the foolish thing of trying to run away from him. I couldn't believe it when I heard my tongue say, "Throw me overboard . . . ." I knew I couldn't swim. I'd never even seen a river wider than fifty feet.

BW: Did they throw you overboard right then?

Jonah: No, the strangest thing happened. I heard them praying to the one true God. Those heathen sailors were recognizing him of whom I was ashamed. God was already where I thought he could never be.

BW: How could a landlubber like yourself still be here to tell about it if the stormy sea was so terrible?

Jonah: Well, as soon as I hit the water, the storm stopped. I looked back up to see the sailors praying to Yahweh and they had even built a crude altar. I wouldn't be surprised if they didn't elect a chaplain within a few minutes.

BW: The part about the big fish is the most unbelievable part. We'll get to that in next week's issue. Thanks, Jonah, for your time.

Jonah: You're welcome, Barbara, but I must insist here that the point of the whole story is not the whale. For me, that's the easy part to believe. What really got to me is the way God was able to rescue me from my own blind culture. I thought he was just the God of a few people. I found out he loves even the ones I don't like.

As an inset on page 6 we read the testimony of an unnamed resident of Nineveh:

Hello, I prefer not to give my name because I don't want you to remember me, but the God I proclaim. I was and still am a resident of the greatest city in the world. There's a lot of civic pride around here, or, that is, there used to be. Now our humble pride is in the Lord. Our city is a large and beautiful one. But, only a few weeks ago that beauty was marred by the grossest of idolatrous sins. As the heart of Assyrian military power, we had learned to rely on our many gods and our own military weight. Incest, sexual infidelity, murder, cheating, and backstabbing were a way of life for us. Our gods were gods of convenience. They sent the good crops, helped our women bear children, and gave us great military victories. We went to sleep at night knowing we were on top of the world and in no danger.

Then a few days ago the Hebrew prophet Jonah came. He cried out with compassion and courage, "Forty days from now you will perish!"

Well, at first we stared in disbelief. Who did he think he was, representing a foreign Jewish god? Then that very God brought our great king to his knees. He proclaimed a city-wide fast as a sign of our willingness to change. Soon we were all in a state of repentance. Overnight the power of God so convicted us that our other gods were seen as weak as they really are.

Our king reminded us that we should remain in a state of repentance for as long as it would take. It did not take long. The one we know now as the one true God saw our acts and knew our hearts. Our city was not destroyed. In fact, we who thought we had a great city know now that we have an even greater one because we are loved.

I haven't seen Jonah lately. The last I heard he was sitting just outside our city gate under a bush of some kind. I wish I could see him. I would thank him over and over for bringing us the good news that God demands justice because he is loving. Someone said Jonah was still mad about something. Maybe when he cools down we can even teach him something about the God he represents. We who love God so much now could possibly help those who have had him so long that they take him for granted. I wonder . . .

Page 7 is a full-page ad with the title "For Sale Cheap: Used Pagan Idols." The page depicts row after row of off-shaped images of winged creatures, half-animal images, and local charms. On the bottom is the line, "Former priests of Ninevite local gods offer these only for their precious metal content. Proceeds will be used to construct a sanctuary to Yahweh. Call after 5 PM as the priests are busy during the day being retrained."

Page 8 is another full-page ad with pictures in the background of clear blue oceans, sand dunes, and manmade towers. The caption reads, "God Wants You!" At the bottom of the page we read, "Call your nearest missionary recruiter. Check on the benefits of taking God to the nations. Teams leave daily. A few special squads will be trained to go to Israel for their prayed-for reawakening. Applicants must be between the ages of 15 and 90."

In the "Architecture" Section is the report on the new altar going up in Jerusalem (Ezra 3).

The new altar at the Temple in Jerusalem has been designed by Ezra-ben-Ezra, Jerusalem's finest. Rumors have it that it will be primarily functional with little attention to ornateness. Simple lines will supplement the basic design. In the words of the architect, "What I am trying to depict here is the simple dignity which the worship of the one true God demands. In Babylon and Persia we were all so affected by the fancy temples and altars. Now we see that the true power and majesty of God are worthy of lines of dignity." All are invited to view the altar on the first day of the seventh month.

The following page has a full-page article entitled, "New Cupbearer Named for Court of Artaxerxes."

With the abrupt departure of Nehemiah only a few days ago, the king Artaxerxes was in a real dilemma. It was shocking news to the rest of the court when the king's favorite was given leave after so many years of faithful service.

The title of "Cupbearer" carries with it great responsibility in the court of Artaxerxes, king of Persia. It is a place of great influence and honor. All Persian royal art shows the cupbearer at the right hand of the king.

It was, then, with a note of sadness that Artaxerxes named one Sandalet to be the new cupbearer.

The next page presents an interview with Tom Snyper of the *Jerusalem Journal* and Sanballat, former leader in Jerusalem.

TS: Well, Sanballat, the past few weeks have certainly been ones of rapid change for you. Only a few days ago you were very influential around here. Then Nehemiah came. How do you see things now?

S: Nehemiah is not being fair to us. It is not my fault that I was born a Samaritan. As you know, when all the young and powerful Jews were taken from this land, someone had to run it. My forefathers came in, took care of things, and held this whole place around here together. It's just not fair.

TS: Some of our readers don't know quite what the term "Samaritan" means. Will you explain it to us?

S: Yes, as we see it, we are the true Israelites, as we are descendants of the tribes of Ephraim and Manasseh. We deserve to be treated as part of the Jewish peoples, not as dogs. It is true that we have intermarried somewhat with others and maybe our worship of God is not as pure as it should be, but why deny us the right to rebuild the walls. That Nehemiah has got to go.

TS: Have you tried to explain all of this to Nehemiah?

S: Yes, of course, but he wouldn't listen. He is so intent on building a "pure" Jerusalem that he might lose some of his most effective help. It just doesn't make sense.

TS: Last week the *Journal* interviewed Nehemiah. He says that the true worship of God has been so polluted in Persia that now no impurities will be tolerated. He takes a hard line, that's true.

S: You're right, but now, what are we to do? If we can't worship here with our own relatives, maybe we'll just go to Gerizim. We'll be welcome there.

TS: You can't be serious.

S: Oh, yes, I am! If what Nehemiah has is so good, why does he not want us to have it? I have been governor here for many years and now I'm rejected for no good reason. If we can't worship here, we'll go elsewhere. I wish we could get along here, though, it would surely be easier.

The next page is the "Religion" Section. The reporter writes:

It has been years since such a controversial prayer has been heard in this land. On Thursday, Nehemiah, former cupbearer to Artaxerxes, who is spearheading the urban renewal project here in Jerusalem, prayed eloquently. In this generation we have had prayers prayed to Jerusalem audiences. Everyone who heard him pray, though, knew it was to God. He prayed in candor:

"Hear, O our God, for we are despised; turn back their taunt upon their own heads, and give them up to be plundered in a land where they are captives. Do not cover their guilt, and let not their sin be blotted from thy sight; for they have provoked thee to anger before the builders" (Neh. 4:4-5, RSV).

For this reporter, it seems that when Nehemiah heard that Sanballat had called a conference of all the former leaders in Jerusalem, he lost his composure. He prayed that his enemies would suffer the same fate that the Jews had suffered, and that God would not forgive them for their sins. Such an emotional outburst is being viewed by some as an understandable response to the provocation, particularly in view of the fact that Nehemiah believed that God himself was offended. But, from this reporter's viewpoint, when pure worship is restored here, it will best be done with love—not vengeance.

In the inaugural edition of the "Women's Page" we read this opinion of our guest writer, Marabel Morganstern, author of *Total Marriage.*

I just don't understand what went wrong. My marriage to Jacob ben-Adam seemed to be going well in spite of the fact that I am an Ammonite. I sent messages to his office letting him know I craved his companionship. I did the bit with the Honey and the curds and whey. We had a wonderful thing going but Jacob kept trying to throw religion into every conversation. I came from a tradition in which we have a god for every occasion. Jacob insisted that there is only one God, called Yahweh, or something like that. That always seemed so narrow, so we didn't talk about it much. Then there were the kids. They decided that having no religion was better than fighting over how to worship.

I still think we could have built a successful marriage, even if we couldn't talk religion, if only Nehemiah had left us alone. When he had the law read, he insisted that all Jews married to foreigners had to leave their wives.

Oh, how he carried on. He tore his clothes and pulled hair from his head, and sat motionless. Then he fell on his face and cried aloud. Who can ever forget these words:

"O my God, I am ashamed and blush to lift my face to thee, my God, for our iniquities have risen higher than our heads, and our guilt has mounted up to the heavens. From the days of our fathers to this day we have been in great guilt; and for our iniquities we, our kings, and our priests have been given into the hand of the kings of the lands, to the sword, to captivity, to plundering, and to utter shame, as at this day. But now for a brief moment favor has been shown by the Lord our God, to leave us a remnant, and to give us a secure hold within his holy place, that our God may brighten our eyes and grant us a little reviving in our bondage" (Ezra 9:6-8, RSV).

Well, I want to tell you that Nehemiah was not through yet. He had a list of "Marriage Offenders" drawn up and my husband's name was on the list, along with most of the people from last year's census. Interfaith marriages were so prevalent it seems to me that Nehemiah was too harsh. I mean, if everybody's doing it, that surely makes it right. And besides, he just got here. Who does he think he is, coming in here as an ambassador for his God and condemning things we have been doing for years.

Nehemiah's compelling fear of religious pollution has broken up my home. With utter disregard for human feelings and human rights both Nehemiah and Ezra have broken up our homes, sent away innocent wives and orphaned helpless children. Why should my generation pay for wrongdoing in another day? Even if I do understand Nehemiah's motives which prompted his action, I do not agree that such brutality is necessary to the preservation of his precious faith. The only thing I can see is that he did what he thought his God wanted.

The next page carries this "Help Wanted" ad:

Help Wanted: Adult "place protectors." Must be available during the daylight hours to stand watch over holes in the city wall. All applicants must bring their own swords, spears, and bows. All interested should apply at dawn tomorrow at the main city gate. Ask for Nehemiah or call 635-2911.

In the "Plants" section we find this notice:

"Worm Epidemic Killing Ninevite Plants"

All plants large enough to supply shade in the Nineveh area were smitten by a yet undiagnosed strain of worms. There are reports that even stubborn and upset Hebrew prophets have been left to the rays of the sun by the destruction of these shade plants.

One religious observer noted that many of the plants destroyed were of an especially large variety. It is believed that the worms may be the black caterpillars native to the area.

When the shade disappeared, one of the prophets was heard to be crying out for his life.

An unnamed Ninevite priest who has recently shifted his allegiance to the Hebrew god Yahweh has observed that in his opinion Yahweh is using this worm epidemic to show the stricken willful prophets the absurdity of their narrow attitudes. The point seems to be that Yahweh is concerned about all of creation, not just the Hebrew peoples. The priest admits that he is new in interpreting the will of Yahweh, but thinks this is Yahweh's way of showing his love for all of his creation. If God is the Lord of all, any narrow exclusiveness of religious thought limiting the scope of God's universal love is doomed to tragedy. When a prophet knows that God's grace and mercy are for all mankind, and yet does not behave accordingly, he is doomed to slow spiritual death. Yahweh wants to save all nations while some missionaries want to see only a few redeemed. God always has the whole world in mind, said the priest. Some of the very prophets who brought the news of Yahweh's love to Nineveh, in their hearts want to reserve his love for only a few. The new Yahweh priest observed that he had learned at least one lesson out of all this: if he preached, it would be out of love for all, not just to have listeners marvel over his powers.

There is no word as to when the worm epidemic will end or how far it will spread. Experts think a lot depends on the prophet's faith and the people's reaction to the epidemic.

This issue of the *Israeli Item* concludes with this editorial, by Pelatiah, resident of Joppa:

I should make it clear that I am a skeptic in religion. So far I have not found a faith with which I can live, but I am still looking. Recently I passed on the streets here in Joppa a Hebrew prophet who was too hurried to talk. It is my understanding that his Yahweh is the one God for all peoples but I am not sure about following a God whose prophets are so hurried.

We got reports that the whole city of Nineveh has turned to this Yahweh. That is almost unbelievable to us because we describe Nineveh as "that great city" and we fear it. The Ninevites have always been famous for their fighting legions. But if Yahweh can change such a city, I would like to know more about him.

Events over in Jerusalem lately have been shocking to a free thinker like myself. I can understand an honest call for purity in religious ritual, but must homes be broken up to obtain such purity? Is there a little jealousy and prejudice in all this hurry to purify religion? Why can't a Samaritan be allowed to worship at a new altar?

That's enough of questions. What I really want to say that the God I would believe in would have to be like this: all-powerful, all-loving, concerned about all peoples, even if he chooses a certain one to do his beckoning to others and, above all, a God who mixes mercy with demands for justice. If there is such a God, I would gladly follow him anywhere. Maybe he has prophets who have time enough to speak to me, even if my mother is a Moabitess. I await such a God and word from his prophets.

Yes, I am looking for balances between purity and exclusivisim, between mercy and justice, between heavenly love and earthly demonstration of it, and between demands for repentance and concern for me. I would even want to be a priest or prophet for such a God. And if I did, I would never represent him as a limited god of my tribe. The only God I will serve is one for all peoples. Then he could be the one for me.

ADDENDUM
Paraphrase of Jonah 2:2-9

(Jonah's prayer in the belly of the great fish)
I am crying out for the one true God out of my panic
And he has not forgotten me
Out of the very pits of hell I screamed for help,
And you remembered my name and my terrible predicament.
It was you who threw me into this vast sea,
And you caused the huge waves around me.
But—because you are loving and when I am not—all of those waves went right around me.
Then I cried out in horror and fright, "I am no longer near you, never again will you accept my worship as genuine."
The waves finally did completely surround me;

The dreaded deep was all over me.

Even in the midst of the mountains at the very bottom of the sea

I thought I was dead because seaweeds were choking me around my throat.

I went all the way down to the land and saw inside the city gates to hell itself.

Yet it was you who brought me up just when I was about to die and enter into punishment.

I was so weak the only one I could lean upon was you.

At the last minute you caused me to call out to you,

And you heard me even all the way up in your heavenly throne room.

Now I know that anyone who bows before anything but you is a fool and has run away from the only true worship.

But I will remember you and offer regular sacrifices to you.

What I have said I will do, for

Only you could save a man clutched in the jaws of hell.

5
Jesus and His Jewish Brothers

Daniel is probably the latest book written in the Old Testament era. It stands as a link to the literature between the testaments. During this inter-testamental period, many Jews tended to become exclusivistic; that is, they wanted to restrict God's good news to only God's chosen people. Jesus came in time to rescue the Jews from such an attitude and to thrust his newly founded church "into all the world."

The book of Daniel stands alone in the Old Testament. It professes to be a history of Daniel, a Jewish young man carried away in exile just before the fall of his native kingdom.

The book is easily divided into two main sections:

Chapters 1—6 contain narratives about Daniel and his faithful companions.

Chapters 7—12 contain the visions of Daniel about Israel's future and are written in the first person.

It is clear that there are allusions in Daniel to the course of events for several centuries following his lifetime. His lifetime is cast in the rule of Nebuchadnezzar, who came to wide power by defeating the rule of Egypt at Carchemish in 605 BC. It was under the same Nebuchadnezzar that the final captivity of the Jewish nation took place in 586 BC. That Babylonian empire lasted until 539 BC, when Cyrus, king of Persia, overran the Babylonians.

The Persian Empire lasted until 333 BC when its final leader was overrun by the forces of Alexander the Great. Alexander died the following year and his dominions were divided. They were finally divided among four of his generals. Finally, the infamous Antiochus Epiphanes (176-164 BC) engaged for Syria in several great battles with Egypt. When he was unsuccessful in expanding his kingdom, he persecuted the Jews with great severity. The Jews resisted his attempts to introduce heathen worship forms among them. His demonic rule led to the successful revolts against him by Judas Maccabeus and his brothers. Their feats are recorded in the books of the Maccabeus in the Apocrypha.

It has generally been supposed that the book of Daniel is the work of a scribe who lived in the time of Daniel himself and recorded these events as they transpired.

Modern biblical scholarship, however, has come up with another view. This modern view is this: the book was written during the time of Antiochus Epiphanes and is based on actual events in the life of the real Daniel much earlier. The aim of the writer was to inspire the Jews to faithfulness in justice and love even under the evil rule of Antiochus Epiphanes. This inspiration will come, the writer believes, when the people hear of the moral strength of Daniel and his friends. This he weaves with the theme of the eminent overthrow of God's enemies, the impending establishment of God's earthly kingdom, the triumph of God's people who remain faithful, and the resurrection of the dead.

Further evidence for Daniel's dating in the second century BC is the author's use of visions and symbols. This is similar to the Apocryphal books of Enoch, 2 Esdras, and the Assumption of Moses. Another point in favor of a late date is that Daniel is the only Old Testament book in which angels are given names (Michael and Gabriel) and special nations are assigned to their care (8:16).

If it is concluded that the book of Daniel belongs to a class of literature unfamiliar to most Protestants, but common to the intertestamental period, we must not conclude that God could not have inspired it. The point of this whole book is that God never abandons his people and never ceases to try to reveal himself to all persons.

The book of Daniel had profound influence on the New Testament. Jesus' pictures of the Son of man coming on the clouds is reminiscent of Daniel (Matt. 13:22). The angel Gabriel appears in Luke 1:19. The last book of the New Testament is highly dependent on Daniel, such as the part played by the archangel Michael (Rev. 12:7).

In spite of its late date, or perhaps because of it, there are numerous lessons for modern missions in the book of Daniel. They include:

1. *God is still in control.*—Bad news floods the air waves in modern America, reminding us of the fact that nations still war against nations, that people do still commit murder and rape and theft, and that money and its value is fleeting. There is hardly a culture to which these factors do not make an inroad. The missionary to Milwaukee or Malawi brings the good news that God still has ultimate control of human events. While God is still all-powerful, however, he does not remove Daniel or the rest of us from circumstances which would call forth the best of our moral courage. God involves us as much in the business of building character and courage as in removing us from moments of hardship.

2. *Faith or lack of it is still a big factor in our fate.*—God is working out his plan in history through us, but only in direct proportion to the degree to which we are faithful.

3. *Guardian angels.*—The view of angels found in the book of Daniel is definitely that of the intertestamental period. In Daniel angels are much more than the conveyors of messages from the Lord. They are beings which control the winds and the seasons. They can affect whole nations in Daniel (10:19-21). They also act as intercessors and guardians of the righteous.

Missionaries continue to report instances in which their lives have been saved in a miraculous fashion. They have felt a special presence of the Lord as if they were supernaturally protected and led to do superhuman feats. Guardian angels may not be present but some events can only be so explained.

4. *Individual resurrection.*—Daniel contains the only clear reference to resurrection in the Old Testament (12:1-2). This is designed in the midst of persecution to be an assurance to the faithful. For Daniel, the message of the future resurrection is that God will reward the faithful. On the other hand, those who are unfaithful will be given over to everlasting contempt.

In many a missionary situation, there are circumstances which make no sense in terms of justice. Only the future can be the scene of complete retribution. That confidence keeps the missionary functioning.

5. *God loves his saints.*—Not even death can remove God's faithful from the presence of his protection. God's call is to death and beyond. Those who refuse to do his bidding because they fear death and dying have not understood that the one who calls is the one who controls.

6. *God operates on his own timetable.*—The patience of a few faithful missionaries in an isolated bush town or in downtown San Francisco is often remarkable. This is partly due to their discovery that God can bless their efforts even after they are gone from the scene. It is God who takes the long look at Christian missions today. His kingdom will triumph in the long run.

7. *God never abandons his faithful.*—There are modern parallels to lion's dens and fiery furnaces. They are not less dramatic. The agriculturalist who takes new seed up-country where he is 800 miles from another missionary discovers that the Son of man goes with him. The nurse assigned to do public health on an Indian reservation discovers that her God is there to overcome the belief in medicine based on fear. God is there as well with the veteran field missionary who watches with a note of pride as the natives take over most of the work.

8. *There is always a place for statesmanship in the life of a saint.*—Daniel discovered that stubbornness must be mixed with wise diplomacy for him to survive long enough to be effective in God's service. There is no need for useless martyrdom or misery when God can be served just as well through a sweet spirit. There is little room for masochism in effective modern missions.

9. *Issues must never be judged by God's faithful servants on the basis of personal danger, risk, or advantage.*—God's call may drive a faithful missionary to fly in the face of all three to serve God. At issue primarily for the one called to be faithful, is what is best for the people served. Daniel exemplified this.

10. *There will always be necessary confrontations between right and wrong.*—Today the church is called to suffer. Her very nature and commission drive her into conflict with human greed, evil, and

selfishness. When she feels no tension with her culture, she has ceased to be the church.

The books contained in the Apocrypha reflect the development of social and religious life among the Jews from about 225 BC to the time of Christ. The word *Apocrypha* means "hidden" and is a collection of fourteen books not generally included in Protestant editions of the Bible. Nevertheless, they help us to understand that God was not dead between the testaments even as today he is active long after the Bible has been written. In these fourteen books we can trace the "ups and downs" of the Jews in the three centuries prior to the coming of Christ. They also help us see how Christ fulfilled the hope God's people retained in trying times, in spite of some who saw God as a Jewish plaything.

An example is the book of Tobit. The story is set in Nineveh. A blind man, Tobit, is healed through the angel Raphael. His son, Tobias, marries a Jewess and she is delivered from an evil spirit. This little tract may be saying that it is better to marry one's own kind.

The short book of Judith also tells a story. Judith is a faithful and beautiful widow who cuts off the head of an evil king. Evidently its purpose is to encourage the patriotic zeal of the Jews in spite of persecution.

The longer Wisdom of Solomon has as its purpose the vindication of the essentials of the Jewish faith against materialism and idolatry. This book had a tremendous influence on the New Testament. One example is the Wisdom of Solomon's description of the armor of the faithful in 5:17-20 and Paul's description of the Christian's armor in Ephesians 6:13 f.

The Prayer of Manasseh is a short confession of personal sin and fervent asking of God-based forgiveness. It purports to be the prayer of the penitent Manasseh, king of Judah, during his imprisonment in Babylon (2 Chron. 33:11 f.). This beautiful prayer poem is a high point in expressing personal responsibility during the period between the testaments.

First Maccabees is a history of the forty-year period following 175 BC in which the Jews carried on their struggle for religious freedom. There is little room given to the miraculous in it. The Jews fought for their very survival against overwhelming odds and they succeeded. It was written by an anonymous patriotic Jew, devoted alone to the maintenance of the customs of his people. He does not even mention the name of God. There is no reference to the growing messianic hope in Israel. This accurate historical survey is just that.

Second Maccabees mentions the name of God often and contains clear references to his personal belief in a resurrection (7:9). He pauses often to exalt the glory of the Lord. Here again, we see a piece of literature aimed at the Jews alone.

The Apocrypha makes it clear that the Judaism between the testaments was being threatened for its very survival. During this 300-year period, the Jews changed their beliefs in numerous ways, indicative of the way a faith can become captive of a culture.

Modern missionaries are often caught in a bind between what is cultural and what is Christian. For example, missionaries in West Africa are often called upon to perform a Christian wedding ceremony in which the bride is very much pregnant. It is the dominant cultural teaching among most West African peoples that the bride must be capable of bearing children before she is worthy of being called a wife. If the missionary refuses to perform such a ceremony, the couple "loses face" in the community and has to have a secular ceremony often because the missionary is the only ordained Christian within a 200-mile radius.

During the intertestamental period, most Jews lost the idea that God is real in their midst. They began to think of God as being transcendent; he was seen as so far above the world that he was cut off from everyday concerns. This led both the Pharisees and the Sadducees in the time of Jesus to resent the familiarity with which he spoke of God as being Father. Jesus had the nerve to describe God as interested in the mundane affairs of all of us.

Most cultures in today's world see their chief god as living above the concerns of everyday life. He supposedly appoints deputies to do his bidding among the common people. To approach him directly is seen to be the height of blasphemy since he is god and not to be bothered with everyday concerns. So, in most animistic religions, sacrifices and other rituals are aimed at a local or lesser god who takes the requests of the people up to the chief god. The New Testament witness to Christ is the opposite of that. Jesus has come to us that we might see God in him. The Christian high God has crossed the space between heaven and earth and made direct access to him possible. That is why the gospel makes sense to so many in the Third World nations today.

The Jewish people between the testaments also put great emphasis on reaching God through the law. Since God had retired beyong the clouds and hidden himself from direct communication with his people, knowledge of him could only be obtained indirectly. Some reasoned that indirect communication could only come by studying the traditions of the past. Since they no longer had his voice speaking directly to them, they had to fall back on the past. In so doing, the more conservative Jews, represented by both the Pharisees and the Sadducees, began to deify the law. Scribes were elevated to the position of great honor and prominence as they preserved that deified post.

Today the least effective missionaries or ministers (both lay and clergy) are those who worship the past. That is easy to see when looking back for a few decades. Early missionaries thought it their duty to clothe the natives in European dress, force them to leave their multiple wives (even if it meant making prostitutes of the later wives), and educate them in the classics of English literature. It is no wonder that the next generation of those targeted for mission thought that surely the Christian God must be just for the white man. The same error, confusing Christ with culture, is not so easily seen today, however. Constantly looking to Jesus Christ as the only foundation for mission, and the Bible as the mirror is the only sure safeguard against such practice.

The intertestamental period saw the rise of giving importance to the individual. Before Daniel, the people as a whole were the chief focal point of mission, with an occasional giant prophet among them called to bring them collectively back to God through repentance. With Daniel we see the emphasis shifting to the kingdom being built through the faithfulness of a few good persons. Jesus and the twelve could therefore be accepted as a workable model for bringing in the kingdom. By the time of Jesus, the individual conscience was to be strengthened by proper teaching. Piety and faithfulness became a personal concern.

The effective modern missionary learns from the intertestamental period by looking back to it through the example of Christ. He called for a group of individual believers held together by a common faith, not merely held together in a political unit. The church was distinguished from the world to enter back into it for ministry. The kingdom Jesus proclaimed was to set brother against brother and son against parents. Today in cultures where the clan is so important, believers in Christ have to be so in spite of great social and religious pressure. One example is in Islamic cultures where persons may be disowned by their families. With sensitivity and concern, the best missionaries operate with caring gentleness in such situations. They realize their Christian obligation to clothe, feed, and house such persons if necessary, who have been cut off from their families. The best missionaries today also have learned that the best definition of the people of God today is one which has a balance between the group and the individual. We serve together best when individual gifts are exercised. It is when the individual missionary knows he is part of the people of God on the move that he is most effective.

Hope for the Jews in the intertestamental period was centered in the coming of a personal God-sent deliverer, who would restore the greatness of Israel. Then God's chosen people would rule in righteousness and power. This helps to explain the effectiveness of the preaching of John the Baptist and the acceptance Jesus received early in his ministry, until he indicated that following him would cost a lot. This hope of the Jews helped to get him killed because when he failed to satisfy their secular and political desires, they killed him. Finally, in AD 70, these secular hopes were dashed with the fall of Jerusalem. Nonetheless, the hope for a personal Messiah intensified in the intertestamental period and should have made Jesus' task easier, had it not been for their selfish schemes.

Today the gospel message is a personal one, molded in the energizing dreams of the Jews just before Jesus. General ideas about unspecific social changes have given way to a specific message: Jesus of Nazareth, Mary's son, is the one for whom we seek. This personal knowledge helps the missionary relate personal need to a person. There is nothing general about Jesus' claims to messiahship. He was what the Jews needed and is what the Ashanti and the Navajo and the Texan need. Because he is personal to so many, he is personal to me. There is no person alive whom he does not seek to love through us.

Finally, the period between the Old and New Testaments saw the rise of belief in life beyond the grave, one in which all injustices will be corrected and all sins forgiven to the faithful. In the Old Testament era, it was believed that righteous and unrighteous alike go to a common grave called Sheol and from which even the most fervent faith cannot deliver. Because God was not dead during the three centuries between the testaments, he led the Jewish faithful to richer and deeper concepts of things to come. They began to affirm glorious life after life. The Jews developed a steadily growing sense of personal immortality. They began to assert boldly the assurance of a resurrection of the body and a godly judgment concerning rewards for the faithful and punishment for the wicked. This was coupled, by the time of the book called 2 Esdras, with the doctrine of a universal resurrection to judgment before God on his throne followed by a life predetermined by the degree of faithfulness to God before judgment. This was the dominant view by the time we get to the ministry of Christ.

The "Book of Wisdom" also reflected the developing concept of punishment for the wicked. Its author wrote, "The souls of the righteous are in the hand of God, and there shall be no torment touch them, having been a little chastised, they shall be greatly rewarded; But the ungodly shall be punished according to their own imaginations." By the time of Jesus, the rabbis had the afterlife neatly divided into two eternal places. Paradise was the place where the righteous were admitted without delay at death. Gehenna was a place whose name was derived from the valley of garbage dumping near Jerusalem. Gentiles and faithful Jews were supposed to go there. Note that only the faithful Jews (not Gentiles) went to Paradise. Even in the afterlife, the devout Jews previous to Jesus' day saw themselves as chosen for privilege.

Daniel and the Apocrypha show a rapidly changing Judaism, one in which faithful responsibility could lead to survival for the people and later for a few individuals. Because of the severe persecution under which they lived, their religion was turned in upon itself. Their concept of other cultures was that they represented "the other" to be despised and feared.

While the modern student of missions can be understandably tolerant of a people under severe persecution, the prophetic emphasis on ministry to all peoples today cannot afford to be so limited, because we follow the Christ who calls all men to him.

Jesus revolutionized the popular Jewish notions of his day when he combined an affirmation and a denial of the cultural and religious mores in existence during his lifetime. That method was proven a valuable one in missionary strategy through the ages. Roberto de Nolili revolutionized Hindu concepts of Christ through adapting the life-style of the Hindu Brahmin during the seventeenth century. He wore the clothes of an Indian holy man and related the gospel of Christ to the values of the Hindu upper classes. His influence permeated an entire culture from the top down. Jesus used a similar technique.

Jesus' teaching concerning the kingdom was an outgrowth of his conception of God which he shared with the Jews of his day. The character of the Father, as he knew him intimately in his own experience, determined for him the character of the kingdom. He challenged the prevalent idea that God was removed from his world, however, by addressing the Father as "Abba."

Jesus also used and amended the popular Jewish notion of the Messiah. At times the Jews thought of the coming one as a reigning monarch, ideal in character and with great power (Isa. 9:6-7). At other times they seemed to be looking for fulfillment within their own role as a redemptive nation by being purified through suffering (Isa. 52:13 f.). In Daniel, the Messiah was presented in terms of the Son of man, sweeping down out of heaven and saving the nation

(7:13-14). In the apocryphal 1 Enoch, the Messiah was considered to be an actual heavenly being (46:3-4).

Jesus used the Jewish people's general idea of a messianic hope as a point of contact on which to build. Gradually God unfolded his own peculiar concepts of the kingdom. One key concept was that the new godly reign would be broad enough to include the Gentiles.

It is clear that Jesus regarded the kingdom as the supreme value of life and the search for it worthy of the believer's whole life. He accepted the traditional hopes of his people that one day God would set up his rule in a new age. When that day comes, God's will is done in every personal and social relationship as well as between believers and their heavenly Father.

Jesus forced the Jews of his day to view the kingdom as broader than just the Israelite nation. God's will, according to Jesus, relates to every aspect of life including riches, race, outcasts, discipleship, forgiveness, love, religious rituals, and true worship. So, Jesus was calling for a new broader ethical and religious community built on faith, not ethnic connections. It would be apolitical in character and the eventual victory of the kingdom was to be ethical, not military.

One chief way Jesus presented the newly proposed ethical kingdom was in the use of paradox. The new kingdom would be both God's and ours, both present and future, both an achievement and a gift, both in the heart and in society, and both gradual and sudden in its coming. All of these paradoxes were designed to take one popular Jewish concept and to expand it into a fuller understanding of God's love. For example, he took the Jewish idea that God was "out there" and reminded them that God is also "right here." Thereby Jesus was reminding them that there is hope in spite of the Jewish deep-seated pessimism. While Jesus employed the traditional symbolism of the Apocalypse to indicate the "other-wordly" and parables to enforce and illustrate the idea that the kingdom of God had come upon men there and then.

Most Jews in the days of Jesus defined love in terms of the Jewish neighbor. But the teaching of Jesus concerning love is vivid and direct which is indicative of the fact that it grew out of his own experience. Jesus knew that love must reach out even to the

Samaritan. Jesus taught that persons should be aggressive in their love for God (Matt. 22:37). Then Jesus added a word from Leviticus 19:18, "You shall love your neighbor as yourself" (RSV). These two statements brought the demands of love together. Jesus reminded his hearers that love toward God and all persons are part of a single love, provided that the first becomes the motive for the second and the second becomes an occasion for realizing the first.

The word Jesus used for love is *agape.* It is far more than weak sentiment. The word carries with it the idea of value and esteem for all persons. Limited agape is not agape at all. Agape reaches out to the poor, the lame, the maimed, and the blind (Luke 14:13-14). Jesus thereby condemned social cliques which excluded the persons particularly in need of open fellowship. To welcome all persons would make for hearty and happy human relations.

There were plenty of surprises in Jesus' definition of the kingdom. His parable of the last judgment (Matt. 25:31-46) has a surprise ending. The destiny of those judged depended solely on the active love they had already shown toward suffering persons. All others who had stressed orthodox belief but who had been less loving in service, were rejected.

Jesus drove his message home by pointing out that sinners, tax collectors, and Gentiles regularly returned love for love (Matt. 5:46-47). Jesus pushed those who thought they were God's people into a deeper and higher form of love (Matt. 5:20). Jesus' aim in teaching unreserved love for enemies was the fullest possible life for both the offended and the offender.

The kind of love Jesus' demands is not passive and sentimental. It is fiercely alive and aggressive. In all of this, Jesus keeps the responsibility of the individual intact. It is up to the individual to decide what invincible goodwill requires, on a situational basis. Jesus added to the growing responsibility of the individual developed between Daniel and Matthew.

In a similar manner, Jesus inherited from his own Jewish people a belief in immortality that has been developing rapidly for more than three centuries. Jesus' teaching upon life after death is found in several situations in the Gospels. For Jesus, the God of the kingdom and the God of the future life were one and the same. That meant that the values in the reign of God on earth were identical with those which prevailed in heaven. For Jesus, the nature of God's kingdom defined the character of eternal life. Today the modern missionary builds his future on that same truth. The life of obedience and joy we know now will continue for eternity.

It was inevitable that opposition to Jesus would develop. He walked in an atmosphere of rigidity in which persons had confused truth with tradition. But, instead of merely conforming to what he found, Jesus faced the situation with a mixture of commitment plus imagination. Jesus refused to let others do his thinking for him. Yet, in all of this he did not seek deliberately to be irritating. He only desired to be honest with himself as he saw himself in relation to his Father.

The situation which developed between Jesus and his religious critics came because the Jews could not be easily wooed away from their religious connections. This was most marked in the occasion which led to the story of the prodigal son (Luke 15:11 f.). Jesus was receiving sinners and eating with them. This they saw as making Jesus ceremonially unclean. Jesus reminded them that missionary love knows no limits and that service is more important than ceremony.

Jesus was no theologian with a carefully developed theological and ethical system. Jesus was an intellectual, but not in the sense of being an abstract thinker. One reason he was such a successful teacher is that he spoke from personal experience. He taught that prayers were answered because his own prayers were answered. He taught that God is love because he knew him as love. Jesus took the best in the religious tradition which he inherited and incorporated it into his daily living. In every case, however, the ideals of the past were accepted as valid for the present only because his own experience confirmed them. The imprint of Jesus' own personality was on every truth he taught. The effective modern Christian missionary operates on the same principle. One shares only what he knows from experience with success. The gospel is best communicated by those who have it in their heart. It is more than abstract principles.

A concrete example of Jesus' departure from popular teaching was his treatment of the subject of angels. The Jewish concept of God in Jesus' day saw him as transcendent. A God who was "high and lifted up" needed intermediaries if he were to keep in touch with his created world. Therefore, God needed angels to do his bidding. Jesus' teachings did not completely omit the mention of angels (Mark 8:38). However, references to angels are not prominent in the teachings of Jesus. That is because Jesus knew his Father to be directly related to the world. Jesus' sense of God was immediate, not coming through angels or other heavenly beings.

When Jesus reinterpreted the Jewish religious notions of his day, it was for the purpose of expanding the Jewish view of their mission. Jesus' kingdom was to be all-embracing. Any tendency to limit was to have the effect of destroying it. No one was to be delivered unworthy of receiving the good news that universal peace is possible.

During the intertestamental period, Jewish theology changed. Jesus used these new ideas as a point of contact in proclaiming the universal kingdom. He gave new meaning to old categories. That method is still valid for modern missions.

ADDENDUM
Paraphrase of Daniel 6:19-23

Then, as a new day broke, the Secretary General of the United Nations came quickly to the pit left by the nuclear holocaust. When he came near the pit where Daniel was, he cried out with curiosity and concern and said, "O Daniel, who claims to serve only the one true God, has your God saved you and you alone from this nuclear attack?"

Then Daniel said, "Oh, Secretary General, my God has saved

me. I am not even scratched or scarred. That is because I have been faithful to him and to you."

Then the Secretary General was amazed and very happy. He commanded U.N. troops to get Daniel out of the pit. Daniel was examined and no scratch was found on him because he had been faithful to God even in the midst of nuclear destruction. Daniel's God was triumphant.

6
The Synoptics' Savior

The first three Gospels in the New Testament are called the Synoptics because they "see together" in most matters regarding the life and ministry of Jesus of Nazareth. They are quite unlike the Gospel of John, which is discussed in the next chapter under the title "John's Jesus: A Portrait."

The first three books of the New Testament, like the rest of the other books in it, have as their central focus the life of Jesus Christ. These three writers were writers shaken by the impact of Christ in their lives. They began the process of writing by compiling certain early Christian confessions of faith. These early confessions were built around the death and resurrection of Christ. That is why more space is given to the final week and death of Christ than to any other feature of his life; for example, Matthew 21—27. The death and resurrection of Christ shaped the subsequent understanding of who Jesus was and how his mission gave impetus to missions. These two events, death and resurrection, in the estimation of his early followers, were central facts in the history of the world. They knew that Jesus' life was the most significant fact for their personal lives. They understood firsthand that the clue to true human living is found in the earthly life of Jesus.

Four components in the life of Jesus serve readily as basics in the formation of modern mission strategy. His life is the only true foundation for missions, therefore it is worthy of serious study.

The first such component in Jesus' life is his ministry. No person ever achieved so much in such a short time as Jesus. In less than three years he founded a church strong enough to withstand strong political opposition.

In the Bible all great men are marked not so much by what they said as by what they did. Jesus performed numerous "miracles" even through the Synoptics do not contain the word *miracle*. Miracle is a modern term, implying a happening in contrast to the known laws of nature. The Gospels speak of "powers," "wonders," "mighty works," and "signs." These "mighty works" of Jesus are not presented in the Synoptics to prove his credentials.

Nearly one third of Mark is devoted to miracles. In all the Synoptics are listed about thirty-five. But, even the casual reader can see that the Gospel writers practiced a remarkable restraint in their reports of Jesus' mighty works. They could easily have multiplied the miracles by developing such broad statements as "He healed all who were sick" (Matt. 8:16).

The miracles fall naturally into four groups: healings, exorcisms, raising the dead, and using natural elements.

Healings abound in the Synoptics. Jesus showed his concern about and power over fever, leprosy, paralysis, dumbness, atrophy, hemorrhage, deafness, blindness, epilepsy, infirmity, dropsy, and a severed ear.

The healing of the leper in Mark 1 is presented in vivid detail as a clear example of Jesus' miraculous power confirming his messianic role. Leprosy, now called Hansen's disease, was a rather common disease in first-century Palestine. The rabbis generally held that leprosy was a direct punishment for serious sins. The rabbis also taught that its healing was as difficult as raising the dead. Victims were shunned for two reasons: contagion and fear of ritual uncleanness. Consequently, lepers were required to live apart from normal society and wear torn clothes. They were required to cry out "unclean, unclean" (Lev. 13:45).

In Mark's account, the leper approached Jesus with a confession on his lips. "If you will, you can make me clean" (Mark 1:40, RSV). Jesus immediately disregarded ceremonial defilement and possible contagion. Jesus reached out and gave immediate healing. The emotional climate immediately worsened. Jesus' compasssion turned into active anger, an emotion he could display readily when appropriate. Jesus' command to be silent about the healing was not obeyed. Now Jesus could hardly enter a city without being surrounded by crowds seeking physical healing.

Today the universal human longing for healing persists. People flock to fly-by-night tent magicians, Christian Science practitioners, and Roman Catholic shrines in search of some kind of relief from physical suffering. The modern missionary who can mix compassion, the listening ear, and referral to competent healers will fare well with the crowds who still clamor for both physical and spiritual healing.

There are only two accounts of raising the dead in the Synoptics. Mark has the raising of Jairus' daughter (5:21-43) and Luke has the raising of the son of the widow of Nain (7:11-15).

Mark relates the raising of Jairus' daughter as set in Jewish territory. Jesus had just crossed the Sea of Galilee by boat. A great crowd gathered about him on the western shore. Then Jairus, a lay president of the synagogue chosen to preside over the services and business, spied Jesus. Jairus fell at his feet and announced that his precious daughter was at the door of death. Jesus dismissed the crowd before he arrived at Jairus' house. He only allowed his three closest disciples—Peter, James, and John—to enter the house with him. A pubic wake was in progress by the time they reached the house. Jesus declared that their sorrow was premature. But, the crowd refused to be quieted because they knew that Jairus' daughter was dead. Jesus entered the death chamber and gave a command. Her response was immediate. She got up and walked. She ate. The miracle was complete. Jesus did indeed raise the dead as a part of his inventory of available miracles.

A third type of miracle account in the Synoptics is nature wonders. The Synoptics have the stilling of the storm, the feeding of the 5,000, walking on the water, and the cursing and withering of the fig tree.

Mark fills his account of the stilling of the storm with concrete details. On the evening of the day in which Jesus had preached his parables from his seashore pulpit, he urged his disciples to go with him to the other side. They then left the crowd. The description of the waves beating against and into the boat is dramatic and realistic. After they cast off, the exhausted Jesus was asleep in the stern on a cushion. The frightened disciples roused him with a stupid question, "Do you not care if we perish?" (Mark 4:38, RSV). When the waves ceased, the disciples were more frightened by the calm than by the storm. They wondered that Jesus was so great that even the wind and the sea would obey him. Any missionary today who goes forth in the power of Christ goes with a force with sway over all that is, including nature. This is especially important to remember when working with persons who follow nature gods.

The fourth category, exorcisms, is the most problematic for modern believers. In most cases, there are four ways used to try to explain away demons in the modern scene. The first of these is that of time. The reasoning goes something like this: there were real demons in the first-century world but not in the twentieth. The logic behind this is a bit weak. What happened to all the demons? Did they get a virus and die when the calendar page turned past the first century? Many psychology textbooks and biblical students still "explain away" such a phenomenon as demons in the time basis, however, in spite of the weakness of this position.

A second common way of explaining away demons in the modern world is by way of geography. It is carefully explained that there are demons in Nigeria and Argentina, but not in the sophisticated modern world. Missionaries are allowed to tell wild stories about deaths due to demon possession so long as the tales are confined to a place far away.

Thirdly, some speakers and teachers deal with demons by allegory. In this system, demons become symbolic of some modern malady, such as lust or drug abuse. The final method of dealing with demons in the modern world is by psychoanalysis of a first-century case study almost two millenia later. The Gerasine demoniac is often analyzed as having unresolved hostility toward his mother or brother-in-law or a victim of a psychogenic disorder of some sort. This final false resolution of the demon issue tends, however, to make Jesus look deceptive. If he had an unusual amount of knowledge of what was real, why did he "go along" with the idea of demons unless they do exist?

This author, based on personal experience, has come to the conclusion that there are demons present in the world today. This gives the Bible more integrity in its witness. When the Bible says there are demons, it means there are demons. This raises several related questions, however. They include:

1. What are demons?

They are entities assigned to do specific evil tasks for Satan against human beings. They are not "evil spirits" haunting man from the grave or spirits of the departed.

2. What is the behavior pattern of demons?

They tend to oppress human beings and tend to inhabit the nearest living being when exorcised.

3. Can a Christian be possessed?

No, because true born-again believers in Christ have already been "bought with a price." However, a Christian can be temporarily affected, mostly by losing Christian joy and other fruit of the Spirit listed in Galatians 5:22 f.

4. What are the symptoms of demon possession?

Basically there are three: a sudden unexplained change in behavior (for example, a faithful, prompt tee-totaling husband arrives home at midnight, obviously drunk, with a prostitute on his arm); a spirit of oppression (some who seek deliverance say they have not smiled for a year or as long as they can remember); and an aversion to religious objects and the name of Jesus or the sight of a Bible is common.

Note: All three symptoms may be present and still no demons are in operation. More often than not there are "normal" explanations for these symptoms.

5. What is exorcism?

The removal of the demons through the power of the Holy Spirit. There are three basic types prevalent in the United States today. They are:

(1) *Traditional Roman Catholic.*—This process involves an officially authorized ordained Catholic priest. (The irony is that Pope Paul VI issued a decree in 1975 declaring that there are to be no longer any official Catholic exorcists. He abolished the ancient Catholic office of exorcist. Therefore, the technique seen in the film

The Exorcist is not official today.) The priest is to read from the "Rites of Exorcism" orginating in the sixth century, AD. Parts of the rite include Psalm 23 and the Lord's Prayer. The priest is to wave a gold or silver cross in the air and sprinkle holy water in the area to ward off danger for himself and the client. This procedure causes the client to be highly dependent on the priest exorcist. For further information on this technique, the reader may want to consult books by Malachi Martin or Morton Kelsey.

(2) *Neo-Pentecostal.*—This process usually involves naming demons and removing them one by one from the client. The exorcist engages in a long and painful battle with the use of such formulae as "I command you in the name of Jesus to be gone . . . ." Numerous sessions are often necessary because while some demons are exorcised in a single session, others remain. The best-known descriptions of this method are found in books by Kent Philpot, Don Basham, and Derek Prince.

(3) *Eclectic.*—This approach to exorcism deals with demons only as a last resort. It seeks to first find other explanations for unusual behavior. The eclectic approach tries to combine the best of approved counseling techniques with exorcism only as a last resort. Insistence is usually made for a medical examination. The counselor-exorcist does this to try to avoid dealing with a brain tumor or other chemical inbalance. The eclectic practitioner usually refuses to do an exorcism until three or four counseling sessions have passed. If he still deems an exorcism session necessary, he may then call in two or three strong men to be present when the attempt is made. The actual exorcism session will be highly client-centered. Usually a Bible passage is read, perhaps Jesus' healing of the demoniac in Mark 5. Group prayer time is then spent. Each person present including the client, prays out loud. Finally, the client is encouraged to so pray the power of the Holy Spirit into his life that there will be no room for evil of any sort left. Ordinarily the client's body will then relax, a smile will be evident, and the cure is complete. There is no built-in dependence on the priest or exorcist.

How much emphasis should be placed on demons in the local church's teaching?

Not very much. The tendency of some insecure people is to be paranoid about the presence of Satan. Much emphasis also tends to reduce the amount of individual responsibility endemic to the Christian life. No power of Satan can be effective without the will of the affected. Overemphasis on the demonic can produce Christians ineffective in witness and ministry because of concern about possession.

Jesus dealt with demons as being real. The church today can do no other and retain integrity with the scriptural witness. Jesus did miracles of all possible types. These four are the major types, but Jesus did it all when it came to the miraculous.

The second component in the life and ministry of Jesus nailing down his role as the only sure foundation for missions is his teaching ability. The Synoptics present the teachings of Jesus from the messianic view. His teachings are memorable today because they were direct and intensely practical. This is also true because they were demonstrated in his relationship to his disciples. Jesus showed through his works that he intensely cares for humans. The Sermon on the Mount shows this clearly. It is a sketch of perfect behavior in a perfect society.

The teaching of Jesus was, above all, authoritative teaching. That authority was inherent in his person. He taught "as one having authority, and not as the scribes" (Matt. 7:29).

More than fifty times in the Synoptics Jesus is called a teacher, more than any other title applied to him in the Synoptics. He has often been called the world's greatest Teacher. But, he did not have the attitude or the training of the professional teacher. He grew up around a carpenter shop. Jesus was therefore a practical man with simple themes: the nature of the Kingdom and the kind of righteousness it demanded. His skills in teaching were extraordinary. This is nowhere more apparent than in the parables he spoke.

Simply stated, a parable is an earthy story with a heavenly meaning. Basically, it is designed for comparison. He used the parable so often that Matthew states that Jesus said nothing to the crowds without a parable (13:34).

Parables teach us even today much that was not originally intended. They picture Jesus as a man of many interests. Nothing was ever too small or too common to escape his attention. His was a fascination for the familiar. When these wide experiences pass through Jesus' focused personality, they become applicable today.

An excellent example of Jesus' use of parables is in the one often called the wise and foolish maidens (Matt. 25:1-13). A wedding took center stage in a first-century Palestinian village. It outranked all other attractions. It was so important that the rabbis often suspended certain religious duties during the period of a wedding. The wedding feast was held at night. The bride's maidens awaited with lamps lighted. Five maidens had an extra supply of oil. Five did not. When the foolish maidens got enough oil, they were denied admittance to the feast. This is a crisis parable. The hour of judgment is always at hand. Modern missionaries at this late hour know that we are nearer Christ's kingdom even than when they were in Jesus' day.

The parables also make it clear that Jesus calls for complete commitment. The clearest indication of this truth is the good Samaritan (Luke 10:30-37). In Jesus' day, loving God was no problem. Most Jews did that well. The real difficulty, as it is today, lies in loving one's neighbor. Missionaries serving now who are on an assignment because they are compelled of God but who do not love their neighbor, Christian and nonbeliever, will not see love do its work of attracting persons to Christ. All ancient civilizations drew the line somewhere. Sometimes the "neighbor" did not include the Gentile, the slave, the divorced, or the foreigner. Today's missionaries who draw the line anywhere will soon fail. The targets of their mission effort will grow wise to their unloving discrimination. The point of the parable is that if a man has love in his heart, it will tell him who his neighbor is. The cost of discipleship is love without limit. Jesus' teaching ability makes this clear. The foundation for missions is the love seen and heard plainly in the Christ-event.

Jesus clearly indicated that judgment belongs to the capable hands of God alone. According to Jesus, the day will soon come when God's will "will be done on earth, as it is in heaven" (Matt.

6:10, RSV). The living and the dead will one day be judged by God. The final separation will be made.

Not all people in Jesus' day were content to leave the task of separation to God. For example, the Pharisees considered those ignorant of the law to be accursed. The Pharisees remained aloof from the ignorant and regarded only themselves as the true people of God. The Essenes went even further. They sought to establish a pure community separated from the normal life of men of their day. Someone, probably a judgmental Pharisee, asked Jesus why he did not separate the sinners from the saints in social activities. Jesus responded with the "parable of the net" (Matt. 13:47-48).

The net of which Jesus spoke was large. Sometimes it was dragged between two boats. When such a net was brought to shore, it contained fish of many kinds. Jesus here is comparing the kingdom to the sorting which follows the fishing. Jesus is saying that disciples are unable to do the separating fairly and efficiently. This is because true and false disciples closely resemble each other in their early developmental stages. Jesus is also saying that the kingdom is God's. He has fixed the time of separation. This time is not here yet.

Missionaries who operate on the premise that they can decide who is lost and who is saved are doomed to failure. They are very likely to be spreading the notion, "If I hadn't come here at great sacrifice, you would have died and gone to hell." That is not good news! The good news is that God is loving us to himself through Christ. A nonjudgmental evangelism will be more helpful in world missions. Leave the judging to God. Only he can handle it. Be a reporter, not a judge.

Jesus, who used parables more than any other method of teaching, rang the notes of certain repetitive themes as he taught. One of these was the Fatherhood of God and human sonship. For Jesus, the essence of the gospel is that God is love and cares with the intensity and impartiality of a father for his children. The brotherhood of man does not make us, in a true sense, the sons of God. It only creates the possibility of such an intimate relationship. There's a deeper relationship available through faith. This deeper kinship is made possible in Christ, who turned the hearts of God's children to their Father. Jesus also taught them to claim their birthright in God. Jesus put into their hands the contract for this deeper sonship. Then he sealed it with his blood.

The ethical teaching of Jesus is based on the idea that this life is a state of preparation for another one to come. He taught that eternal rewards wait until another life. Pain and injustice are made bearable by knowing they are part of a cleansing discipline by which God is preparing his sons for eternity. Christ taught that in the future, the faithful will live in a glorified universe (Matt. 19:28). Jesus paints the picture of heaven as a perfect society based on unlimited love. It is for and toward that perfect society that all modern missionaries are marching.

The model of teaching for all persons since Jesus spoke the words is the 107 verses today usually referred to as the Sermon on the Mount. Central to this master discourse are the Beatitudes. The character demanded here is strikingly similar to that of Jesus himself.

The term *blessed* may be translated, "How happy!" The last of the Beatitudes is perhaps the one most applicable to the modern missionary: "Blessed are those who are persecuted for righteousness' sake, for theirs is the kingdom of heaven" (Matt. 5:10). If persecution is invited for such a reason as self-glory, it does not qualify for righteousness' sake. The teaching here is that those who experience hardship, suffering, or persecution while serving God are the truly happy ones. Modern missionaries are able to endure culture shock, deprivation of modern conveniences, and separation from families precisely because they believe God's promises. They are not to be pitied or glamorized. They are simply the ones who have discovered the secret of Christian happiness.

Jesus describes life in the kingdom in the Sermon on the Mount. In his saying on murder, Jesus let it be known that he is just as concerned about cause as consequence (Matt. 5:21 f.). Jesus was concerned with motives, known finally only to God. On adultery, Jesus warned against treating a woman as a passing pleasure rather than a person. On divorce, Jesus taught that marriage is permanent and that love does not lend itself to legislation. On prayer, Jesus counseled that all prayer be addressed to God rather than to the crowds. On fasting, Jesus called for faces of gladness, not sadness. Then the fasting and the fasters will be approved of God, not of other believers. On possessions, Jesus knew that a human's interests are where his investments are. The possessor becomes the possessed. In the end, the world's goods do not remove anxiety. Rather, they increase anxiety. On prayer, Jesus counsels humility and persistence.

The Sermon reaches its epitome in the Golden Rule and the Model Prayer. Each is reflected in the other. For Jesus, God was not a cold and impersonal power. To Jesus, the Father was a loving, concerned, responsive, redemptive person whom Jesus knew intimately. This heavenly Father bases his forgiveness on our willingness to forgive others. His forgiveness is not limited *to* our forgiving, it is limited *by* it. An unforgiving and uncaring spirit shuts the door in God's face and in the neighbor's face. Any missionary who combines the attitude of prayer with concern for the neighbor is likely to be successful in both the areas of vertical and horizontal relationships. In all the Sermon on the Mount, Jesus stresses that humans are more important than any religious rules or rituals. A missionary who forgets that basic truth is likely to shake the only sure foundation of missions—Jesus' life and teachings.

The repetitive theme in all of Jesus' teaching is the kingdom of God. The Christian missionary simply lives in another frame of reference when it comes to attitudes and actions. His rules are laid down by the Lord. Jesus promised happiness to those who view life as he does. "Blessed are the eyes which see the things that ye see" (Luke 10:23 f.). That happiness is built on the realization that the kingdom is not a renovated social order produced by human effort. That takes the pressure off of anyone doing the "work of the Lord." Stress disappears when the faithful missionary sees that his efforts are honored by the ultimate godly power behind the kingdom. The kingdom is a divine act, not a divine demand. It is God's rule becoming effective anywhere in the world of human experience. It is a Christian teaching religious knowledge at a foreign university. It is a missionary doing surgery by the light of a flashlight at a bush medical clinic. It is a home missionary bandaging a knee on a playground during a Saturday afternoon skate time. It is God in action, through Christ and his followers, for the salvation and wholeness of human beings. It is the essence of Christ in action.

Jesus, the Master Teacher and personal foundation for Christian missions, had much to say about himself and his former and present role as Savior. The most important christological verse in the New Testament is Matthew 11:27 (author's rendition):

> "All things have been delivered unto me of my Father,
> And no one knoweth the Son, save the Father,
> Neither doth any know the Father save the Son,
> And he to whomsoever the Son
>   willeth to reveal to him."

In this verse Jesus claims not only to be the instrument of God's self-revelation, but also that he alone knows God truly as Father and because of that supreme knowledge all persons must become debtors to him. This is his "unshared sonship."

The title Jesus used to describe himself more than any other was "Son of man" (Mark 8:31). The dominant idea in that title was lordship. Jesus was saying that he was the bearer of godly rule. Modern missionaries need to recall, however, that Jesus combined the idea of sonship here with service and sacrifice. We are not so much to rule but to serve.

Jesus assumed many powers he had during his use of self-imposed titles. The first was his claim that he could forgive sin. Jesus was one who knew himself to be uniquely authorized by the Father. Jesus knew that whenever he acts, God is acting. If any simply mortal man had made this claim, he would have been labeled insane. The most important need for all mankind today is forgiveness. The guilt load of moderns is a heavy one. Jesus crosses cultures and the centuries of time with that needed forgiveness wherever ministers in his name are there as emissaries.

Those who minister as missionaries today are vitally interested in what Jesus said of the future in his day. We are living in that future now. The first clear truth is that Jesus forecast suffering for himself and his followers. He put this truth in the contexts of the day of judgment and the triumph of the Son of man. The truths that Jesus rose from the dead and will rule in the future over all mankind keep modern missionaries functioning. The suffering of the present is just a sign of the future reign which is coming.

The third component in Jesus' life which aids in forming modern missions strategy is his sinlessness. Jesus lived beyond sin in spite of the fact that he was tempted with power and pride more than any human. The temptation accounts in the Synoptics are but signs of temptations which followed Jesus throughout his ministry. Jesus denied Satan a kingdom built on bread. Later, he denied the evil one the suggestion that he challenge God and fail to trust exclusively on him. He fought his way through all temptations to follow on a clear vision of his messiahship. Jesus' sinlessness stands as an inspiration to all who struggle for integrity while being human and striving to serve in his name. It can be done! To be human does not necessarily mean to succumb to sin on a regular basis. There was nothing partial or artificial about the humanity of Jesus. He was no Walt Disney cartoon character faking a human facade. When he hurt, he hurt intensely. When he bled, it was real blood. When he died, he was dead. Human frailty was his lot and he did not count it as a negative factor. All who bear human flesh as missionaries succeed in direct proportion to their dependence on the sinless One.

The fourth component is the Synoptics' view of Jesus' life which qualifies him as our foundation for missions is that of his revolutionary character. Jesus' words: "But I say unto you" repeated often finally got him crucified. He was too hot to handle in a world uptight about sameness. The Pharisees were trying to turn Jesus into a political revolutionary but he rejected that role for the one of inside revolutionary. Jesus came after the hearts of humans. He knew that actions change when attitudes change. Wherever missionaries serve to change attitudes toward God and others, they serve in the tradition of the one who was unafraid to challenge rigidity of religious ritual. Revolution follows his followers today. It is apparent wherever missionaries have been and makes itself known in education, medicine, social action, and inward peace. The revolution continues.

These four components in Jesus' life qualify him for providing foundational strength for modern missions. The Synoptics' Savior lives anyplace where his teachings, miracles, revolutionary character, and sinlessness are emulated. The result is the timely and timeless service to God's children, and God smiles.

ADDENDUM
Paraphrase of Mark 5:1-20

Jesus and his closest disciples had just crossed the Arizona desert when they came into Los Angeles. When they came to the edge of Beverly Hills, there met them a man who had been the route. He had dropped acid, been to an EST weekend, tried Zen, and shaved his head. All the people called him a weird dude or an off-the-wall fruitcake. He was forced to spend most nights at the Salvation Army. He had been in and out of prison so often that he wore mostly prison uniforms. The people had tried almost everything to control him, including Methadone and Alcoholics Anonymous. Both by night and by day he was a continuous embarrassment to the whole community.

When he saw Jesus, the weird man fell at his feet and worshiped him. He spoke with a voice obviously not his own and said, "What do you want with me, O Son of God? Please don't bother me!" Jesus did not really believe in demons because he had read Jung and Freud. He called Andrew aside and said, "These people believe in demons but that's only because they are primitive savages. I'm going to go along with their superstition because they don't understand that what we're dealing with here is unresolved hostility in this man toward his brother-in-law." (Jesus could not get the attention of Peter because he was always talking, being the Howard Cosell of the disciples.)

Jesus said, "What is your name?" The voice from within the man replied, "We are Mob, because we are so many." The voice begged Jesus not to bother him. Nearby there was a bunch of dogs. The voice said, "Send us into the dogs." The spirits inside went to the dogs! The dogs ran into traffic and were killed. The local Humane Society protested. (They didn't care about humans until some animals got hurt.)

A large crowd gathered. Suddenly they noticed the formerly weird dude sitting quietly. Then the crowd got really frightened. A few began to whisper about what Jesus had done. The crowd demanded that Jesus leave that neighborhood. Jesus turned to leave but was stopped short by the healed man. He wanted to leave with Jesus. Jesus told him to go home and make peace with his parents and siblings. The not-so-weird dude told everyone in Beverly Hills about Jesus and his power and love. Jesus winked at Andrew.

7
John's Jesus: A Portrait

The Gospel of John has special emphasis not found in the Synoptics. One of these is the sonship of Christ. Jesus is the "only son" in John; that is, unique and in a category all by himself (John 3:16,18). While in such a unique category, Jesus is also fully human. This is shown in such ways as becoming tired and thirsty at Jacob's well (4:6). In John, the Incarnate Savior possesses a truly human spirit and was subject to many types of painful human experiences. He wept (11:35) and was troubled (v. 33). In John, the Father places his stamp of approval on the Son by bearing witness to Jesus (5:17). Also, the Father allows his own power to reside on and in Jesus.

Uniquely also, the Son is eternal; that is, he was at the very beginning of all that is (1:1). The Son returns to the Father from whom he has come (14:1-3). It is John who emphasizes the unity of Christ's person and the unbroken stream of his consciousness reaching back beyond the incarnation into eternity (17:5). This sonship qualifies Jesus as the uniquely designed foundation for modern missions.

The main object of the Fourth Gospel is to present Jesus as the Messiah and the Son of God and thereby to elicit faith in him. Among the leading religious ideas of the Fourth Gospel are: "eternal life" as a present and a future possession; the "new birth" or birth from above of water and the Spirit; "truth" in the sense of holiness which ought to go along with true belief (17:17) with the accompanying phrase "to do the truth" (3:21); a contrast between "light" and "darkness" in the spiritual sense (12:35-36); "witnessing" to religious truth being affirmed of the Father (5:32 f.) and of the Son (3:11) and of the Holy Ghost (15:26).

Among the titles of Christ peculiar to John's Gospel are the Word (1:1), the Light of the world (8:12), the Good Shepherd (10:11), the

Way, the Truth, and the Life (see 14:6), and the Holy One of God (see 6:69).

John develops the idea of the Holy Spirit more than the Synoptics. His functions are made clear (16:8,13-14).

For John, God the Father is unknowable unless and until he reveals himself through his Son (7:28-29). The obvious reason for God's revelation through his Son is his love for the world, of which he is Creator and Redeemer.

The incarnate Christ is given the title Son of God much more freely in John than in the other Gospels. John also stresses that Jesus is king much more explicitly than do the other evangelists (18:33 f.).

In John, the result of Jesus' earthly ministry is to call into being a body of believers who are to be united through the Son to the Father (17:21 f.). They are called a flock of which Jesus is the Shepherd (10:11 f.). The bond which unites them to each other and to the Father is love (14:21). It is those who respond in love and faith to the love of Christ shown in his death who will enjoy the gift of the Spirit as a personal presence (7:39). When Jesus is no longer present in a physical form, the Spirit replaces him (14:16-18).

There are six signs in John leading up to the seventh and final sign, the death and resurrection of Christ. The first sign, the changing of water into wine, symbolizes Christ's ministry. The second and third, two miracles of healing, show Christ as the bringer of life and forgiveness; the paralyzed man by the pool and the miracle of manna. The fifth is the curing of a blind man and illustrates that "in him is life." The sixth, the raising of Lazarus, shows Christ as victor over death and presigns his own resurrection.

Nowhere more than in John's discussion of the Logos (Word) do we see W. O. Carver's definition more clearly portrayed. Dr. Carver defined missions as "The extensive realization of God's redemptive purpose in Christ Jesus by means of human messengers." As the Logos of God, Jesus of Nazareth was God's ultimate human messenger.

In Jesus as the Word, we see love at its human limit. In Christ we see that love is joy and satisfaction in the other and that love is freedom for the other. We see also that love is creative concern for the other. Love never sits still and waits for the neighbor to come and beg for help. In Christ we see seeking love. Any missionary who has risked his life and spent his life helping others does so in the realization that he is following after the Word made flesh. He knows that in all practical matters, love is all that matters.

The love found in Christ as Word transcends all cultural barriers. It goes beyond being color-bound or color-blind. It is color-rich; that is, seeing differences but escaping the chains of prejudice which the evil world tries to superimpose. This is because it is known through John's Gospel that the Logos is God's outgoing nature creating community.

The fact that the Word became flesh is the living proof that there can be no genuine presence of God that is not a living presence. After the Word has dwelt among us, God is not known as ultimate principle or any other impersonal category.

In Christ we find the Logos which is ahead of and beyond all religion and religions. The Logos is for all persons in all religions. It calls for all humans to come out of their religious traditions to meet the living God. That personal knowledge gives every missionary the right to point the way out of religious bondage to the living Lord. This is also because the God we find in the fleshly word is ever recreating new processes to come out of old patterns.

The Word shows us that God is a gathering God. He gathers from the past for the future and from tradition to relationship. The love set loose in the Word never dares to escape back into the past or future. It is content to live in the present because it has met the Lord of both yesterday and tomorrow. Time is viewed differently in most Third World cultures. When the missionary grows impatient at a late-starting worship service or an unkept appointment, he manages to retain some degree of gentleness because he has met the Master of time and space. This allows him to rest comfortably amid strange sounds, smells, and sights and under foreign skies.

The Gospel of John, according to most biblical experts, is especially suitable as a modern missionary manual because it is aimed at Gentiles. It was probably the latest Gospel, written about AD 90, after the early church had started to reach out to non-Jews. It was written from Ephesus and was obviously intended for Greek readers. Two clues are that Aramaic words are translated (9:7) and Jewish customs carefully explained (4:9).

"The Jews" come in for some sharp words from John (12:37 f.). He strongly reacts against any Greek tendency which might view the humanity of Jesus as a mere appearance. Jesus' humanity is upheld as John is aware of his intended Greek readers. Anyone today who wants to take the gospel across cultural lines can learn a few lessons from John. He takes time to explain what may not be easily understood. He retains the best from his own tradition without being uncritical of its weaknesses. John is perfectly willing to denounce problem areas in the culture he is trying to reach. He has taken the time to learn much about his target audience while not forgetting or abandoning his own traditions. John's Gospel is a model of transcultural communication.

John begins with his now-famous prologue. The first eighteen verses form an introduction to the Gospel. He begins with a hymn to the Word which also provides a summary of what is to come. There are three main ideas contained in the prologue and in the remainder of the Gospel. They are: Jesus is the personal revelation of God (vv. 1-14); the specific work of Jesus was to give life (v. 4); and this life is possible only through union with Christ (vv. 12-13).

John knew that in the religions of his day (as well as today) there is found the idea of some intermediary vehicle whereby God reveals himself to the human family. The Greeks of John's day had such an idea, except that their "Word" also meant "logic." They felt that there was a reasonable force that ruled and directed the course of the world. John built on that idea by announcing that the Word after Jesus is to be thought of as personal, seeking to relate to us. The Word, according to John, does not simply stand face-to-face but exists on an eternal living relationship. All emissaries of Christ today can walk with confidence into any culture that values logic and announce that Jesus wants to be real with them on every level of human knowing.

In verses 2 and 3 of John 1, the author deals with the part played by the Word in the world's creation. It is John's thesis that through Christ all existence came into being. John is trying to deal with the common idea that God needs an intermediary of some sort to create and sustain the world. Jesus and the Father are so merged in John's theology that Jesus is not an intermediary on assignment but an actual part of the Godhead. The implication of this is far-reaching for missionary activity. The emissary for Christ is not representing a simple dying-and-rising Savior motif common to the Middle East (although the physical resurrection of Jesus is unmatched). The missionary is the ambassador for the very one who created and now sustains every facet of nature, including every person in every culture. The Gospel message then becomes partly, "I would like to introduce you to the very one who made you."

John 1:4 continues the creation motif except the tense shifts to the present. The creation which came to life through Christ now daily springs back to life in him. This power is only a possible one; however, it is not automatic. Through faith exercised by the human element of creation, Christ's power is released in the cosmos. So, the witness elicits faith in order to release dynamic power in the world, the only kind of power in which humans can expect to find world and inner peace.

In verse 5, John is saying that there is, unfortunately, moral evil loose in the world so that Christ's power is currently unavailable. That evil John calls "darkness." A good translation might be, "The darkness pursued the light but found it invisible." No one who has struggled to witness to the powerful force of Christ's love doubts the existence of that moral evil. It is often personified in tribal leaders who resist the gospel. All who have witnessed can also testify to occasions when the gospel has overcome that darkness. The struggle continues while missionaries carry flashlights.

Verses 6 and following seem to be an interruption in the prologue, but they form a valuable interlude for the modern missionary. The motive of these verses is an obvious one; that is, to assert the superiority of Jesus to John. The original context was probably a sect in Ephesus still holding to the baptism of John. Today's context is that any missionary who forgets, and the temptations to do so are multiple, is not Jesus. There is, surely enough, a mystical identification with Jesus which Paul calls "Christ in you." But, there is a fine line between representing God and pretending to be God. The missionary who forgets that, can find himself in the "Jim Jones" syndrome. John the Baptist was not Jesus. Neither are we, even when the temptation to play God comes because of geographical isolation or vocational stress. John the Baptist shows forth a borrowed glow. Jesus is still the light. John's role is to stand aside and point potential believers to Jesus. Our roll is the same.

Verses 12 and 13 combine to remind the readers that the only source of true life is God himself. Those who seek life outside him are simply shadowboxing. Here John's emphasis is similar to Paul in Athens as recorded in Acts 17:23, Whom therefore ye ignorantly worship, him declare I unto you." Thus, the missionary today is to view with gentleness the person's pilgrimage previous to the witness event. One simply takes persons where he finds them and points them to Jesus as the Light.

John 1:14 is the crux of the prologue. The word used here for "flesh" is the usual Greek term for the total human personality. John is asserting that the preexistent and co-creator Christ has freely chosen to identify his total personality with real human flesh. There is no game-playing here. Modern missionaries follow in the pattern of he who made this the "visited planet" with his total personality. Any missionary who so fragments his own personality or the personality of any person he works with is not in the pattern of Christ. Jesus demands total obedience to all the personalities in the world.

John also tells us in verse 14 that Jesus did more than pass through this planet earth. The word John chose may be translated "tabernacled." This is a term implying Divine presence. This helped to make the Christ-event unique.

John uses the term "glory" to describe that unique Divine presence residing in the person of Jesus. He uses the same word here that is in the more familiar John 3:16. It is usually translated "only begotten." John's use here is that Jesus is united to the heavenly Father by a bond of mutual love, supreme and unique. This means that Jesus was fully God as well as fully man. There was never any diminishing of either aspect of his personhood. John is saying here that the totality of Godness is summed up in Jesus. That makes it possible on a daily basis for Christians to receive "grace stacked up on grace," as waves follow one after another in the ocean. From Christ's fullness of Godhead all this flows. Thus, the missionary receives daily from the overflow of God's fullness in Christ enough grace to do his task and enough inner power to do the impossible.

In verse 17 Jesus of Nazareth is mentioned by name for the first time. The contrast is between Moses and Jesus. Moses received the law for a set of particular circumstances and for a time sequence. The gospel in Christ comes to satisfy needs in human nature wherever and under whatever conditions it is found.   Most persons in today's world live under a partial revelation designed, they think, only for their tribe or society. The miracle of the gospel is that it is tailor-made for every person in whatever age he is living. The prologue ends. History begins. John is certain that history will support what he has said about Jesus theologically. Whenever human misery is made easier in Christ's name, history is proving that the gospel is more than words.

In John 3 there is found the familiar story of Nicodemus's midnight visit to the historical Jesus. He is symbolic of all who seek him from within the dark veil of religious tradition. Today more than one billion live a superimposed Communist life-style. They are joined by the 800 million Muslims and 500 million each of Buddhists and Hindus. One third of a billion live under what might be called animism. Religion is still a deterrent to many who grope in darkness for the Light. If missionaries wait until they find persons with no religion to witness to, they will wait in vain. It is interfaith witness that Jesus was doing that night with Nicodemus. Interfaith witness requires a knowledge of the other's tradition as well as one's own faith. Jesus shows that he has both in order during this entire interview.

When Nicodemus and Jesus met, Judaism and Christianity were in the early stages of being rivals. Nicodemus was perhaps there that night to test the claim of a would-be prophet. This was one of the functions of the Sanhedrin. He may have been there in an official capacity. By the time John wrote the Gospel, Judaism and Christianity were in full-blown warfare for the allegiance of persons in the first-century Roman world. Therefore that interview was of more than a passing interest to his first readers. Similarly today the demand for the necessity of a new birth is one met with opposition for some already with a strong religious tradition. The witness should note, therefore, the combination of gentleness and firmness with which Jesus insisted on the necessity of the new birth.

In verse 2 Nicodemus acknowledges the good work of Christ without personally identifying with it. There are few people in any culture who reject Jesus outright. There are few who despise and reject him. Most people in today's world are like Nicodemus in that they admire and reject Jesus. To this member of the Sanhedrin, Jesus was an acknowledged religious prophet to whom he was not ready to give his allegiance. He was still gathering data. He was not ready for a relationship. Jesus was an object to him, not a subject. It seems later, however, that Nicodemus came to admire and accept Jesus in full lordship. Jesus' ability was in strong insistence on the new birth while taking advantage of Nicodemus' interest in him. That is precisely what the present-day witness does. He is seeking to turn those who admire and reject Jesus into those who admire and accept his lordship.

It is evident in verse 4 that Nicodemus is missing the point of Jesus' saying because he is viewing the words as being literal. Here Jesus is speaking in parables to increase the interest of Nicodemus. What Nicodemus was trying to cast into a literal, legalistic mold, Jesus was "spiritualizing." The relaxed atmosphere in which Jesus conducted his ministry made his efforts more profitable. He was never uptight. This factor helped Nicodemus open up. When Nicodemus expressed doubt, Jesus kept on his singleminded tract by defining the conditions of the new birth upon which he was insisting. Jesus was calling for a complete transfer of inner nature. No patchwork logical approach would do. Jesus was emphasizing that through logic alone one cannot know the mystery of the new birth. To explore fully the ways of the Spirit is as impossible as tracing the footprints of the mind. Nonetheless, nothing short of everything will do when following God through Christ. He insists on the whole heart, mind, and soul. Nicodemus was trying to keep his faith in his neat logical compartment where he felt comfortable. Jesus was pushing for temporary discomfort which was bound to result in future inner peace. Missionaries may on rare occasion wonder whether temporary disruption of a culture's traditions are worthwhile or necessary. The point of this interview is that partial presumptions must be challenged.

John 3:8 reminds the current witness that the "wind bloweth where it listeth." In this day in which discernment of the Spirit is mandatory, some guidelines are necessary. The Holy Spirit today is wherever three conditions are met: persons are being helped, the name of Jesus is being glorified, and the biblical injunctions are being followed. At times talk about Jesus is cheap, but persons are not being aided. Secular humanism produces the door-to-door salesman of light bulbs for the Lion's Club but the name of Jesus is not being verbalized. The Bible serves as the mirror for missions by keeping the balance between social ministry and evangelism, between the verbal and the physical. The Spirit of God, like the wind, is self-creative and accountable to itself alone. It is the unwise steward who does not understand that God's work is done at his speed and in his chosen times and places. Those unable to "hang loose" in the Spirit while doing missions are doomed to exist in the rigidity which kept Nicodemus from believing at first.

Nicodemus now grows silent as Jesus begins a speech. He contrasts events which can be seen by ordinary human instruments and those only known through divine revelation. The concept of heaven is brought to earth by Jesus and he equates the kingdom with the amount of faith the potential disciple has. Belief then becomes central in verses 15 and 16. For John, to believe is to combine the intellect and the will. There is no anti-intellectualism here. The intellect can go only so far, however. Then the required faith takes over. Similarly, when one believes in Jesus, it is in the eternal dimension, beyond mere logic. Through faith in Christ one enters into the eternal dimension of life, beyond normal human comprehension and experience. John 3:16 continues the thought by stressing that God's love is limitless but available only to those who have faith. Note that Jesus died for "the world." There is not one aspect of human life which Jesus does not desire to be Lord over. He has paid the ultimate price for that lordship. He took upon himself human flesh but then was willing to give it up. Anyone who seeks, in Christ's name, to limit the gospel to one segment of any population, is simply not operating on Christ's level.

Eighty percent of the world's population today is not Christian. John 3:18 teaches that such persons are condemned already because they are self-condemned. So, God's final judgment is only the consummation of a process that is already going on. Those who wallow in ignorance and unbelief already stand condemned. The Judge, in the person of Christ, will simply confirm the clear verdict that unbelievers have already pronounced upon themselves. It is this which lends a sense of urgency to the present missions tack. The coming of Christ has compelled persons to choose for or against eternal life. The choice is no longer a nice option. It is mandatory for every person in our world.

This truth makes it an urgent task to witness of the Christ to every person living. It does heighten the responsibility of every person who hears but also the opportunity of hearing. The idea that the gospel need not be preached because in hearing it some will reject and therefore be sent to hell is not within the New Testament sphere of witness. The witness speaks out of the realization that those who do not believe already live within a sphere of darkness. The Light comes to shine its way into that darkness. It is true that God will hold all responsible for whatever degree to which they have been exposed to the gospel but this does not imply that they are above judgment now. They are being judged as in darkness. Exposure to the Light of the world gives them an opportunity to escape that darkness.

Jesus' treatment of the Samaritan woman at Jacob's well as recorded in John 4 is a classic case study for how to do missions. Here we see Jesus in contact with a non-Jewish people. Jesus himself seems to be anticipating in this incident the extension of the

Christian church beyond the ethnic boundaries of Judaism. He does not draw any boundaries or limits to his love. He speaks to a woman. No self-respecting rabbi would have treated a woman as capable of learning. They were forced to sit in a corner at synagogues if not forced to stay outside. Yet Jesus treated this woman as if she had spiritual worth. Today women all over the world are experiencing a revolution in worth and value. But, some are oblivious to the greatest force for women in the history of this world; that is, the way Jesus treated women. He never scolded a woman for being feminine. He never looked down at one for being female. He treated them as persons of worth and dignity. Finally, he died for woman. It is a puzzle to most students of the Bible that so many women remain outside Christ when he offers them so much.

In John 4:6 we find a tired and thirsty Jesus who sat down just as he was. Jesus got to the well about noon, when the sun was the hottest. He sweated and glinted in the sun as the real man that he was. In verse 7 Jesus asked for a drink because he was just plain thirsty. He also did so because he knew that one way to gain the attention of any person is to ask a service from him. Human missionaries are not afraid to admit their humanity. They go to be ministered to as well as to minister. In admitting their weaknesses they become strong. New Christians in foreign lands want little more than to be loved.

The woman at the well knew very little about heartfelt religion. All she had been able to pick up is that some folks are divided. She was amazed that Jesus went against both religious and social mores by speaking to her. She was one of the first to discover that Jesus is more interested in redeeming human beings than in observing religious taboos.

In verse 10 Jesus shows himself as master of transcultural redemption. He finds a point of contact whereby he can meet the woman's true spiritual needs. He asks for water because he will soon offer "living water." The water he offers is in sharp contrast to the muddy stagnant pool that the woman is preparing to dip. Jesus spoke to this desert-dwelling woman about water. To a modern stockbroker he would speak of tickertape. That is because he is the perfect model of relating to persons where they are and taking them from that point to redemption in him.

In verse 13 Jesus makes it clear that the water of which he speaks is of another kind. Jesus offers a spiritual banquet that will banish thirst forever. She was still thinking of water which only quenches the thirst of the moment. Jesus' water is eternal in time and quality. Jesus' witnessing technique shows that he knew how to excite the desire for spiritual good and is also able to satisfy it. What only Christ can give is an eternal fountain that gives to the Christian believer a source of inward life. That life springs from the Holy Spirit in ever-fresh development.

In verse 16 Jesus boldly says, "Go, call your husband . . . ." Therein he confronts her with the shady side of her personal life. Jesus never avoids confrontation with any person's basic problems. In fact, his penetrating living water is available only to those who open their inner being to Jesus. The woman responded by showing that she was not ready to repent. She tried to talk religion. There is a world out there where people would much rather consider religion than repentance. But, Jesus kept the pressure on and pushed until the woman was ready to repent. Jesus kept driving her back to the realization that it is not the place where we worship but the spirit in which we worship.

In verse 21, Jesus is saying that all sectarian rivalries are forgotten as the believers get closer to the heavenly Father. Allegiance to him and emulation of his Spirit leave little room for fussing about little differences such as the place of worship. Jesus at once openly confessed himself as a Jew but claimed superiority for his faith and demands of obedience. American missionaries are successful in foreign cultures only to the degree they admit their Americanization of the gospel and their willingness to overcome it for the sake of the gospel. When the body of Christ is universal, titles like "American" and "African" Christians have no relevance. The adjectives give way to the nouns and verbs in the Christlike church. In that future day God will be worshiped "in Spirit"; that is, as he really is. To that end present-day missionaries are helping to overcome intermediate barriers and symbols.

Unity in the body of Christ will be realized when attitudes and information picked up are no longer conditioned only by those natives who speak English. For many years, American missionaries could get by with cultural blindness and linguistic ignorance. All this is past. American dollars no longer buy friendships. The unity will come when love replaces any sense of tyranny and air of superiority. It can come in this generation.

In John 5 one can see clearly that religion for Jesus in John's Gospel is not restraint or ritual but life itself. Here we read John's account of the blind man healed on the Jewish sabbath. Herein outworn legalisms are replaced by the gospel of life.

The man Jesus healed had been lame for almost a lifetime. The mention of the length of the man's illness serves to emphasize Jesus' love and courage in healing on the sabbath. Jesus asked whether the man wanted to be saved because the human will must cooperate with the divine in all "faith healing." The Pharisees did not care that the man had been healed. They only cared that the sabbath had been abused. To them sets of religious rules were more important than removing human suffering. They were not concerned with the cure, but with the timing.

The healed one gave testimony to Jesus' ability to do counseling, healing, and forgiving. Today there is much talk about holistic healing. No one brings that technique as new to Jesus. He knew the value of total healing long before Americans heard of psychosomatic disorders.

Jesus shocks the narrow Pharisees by claiming that he is an extension of the healing activity of the heavenly Father. He declares that this unique relation to God makes him "Lord of the sabbath." There is nothing in John's Gospel that Jesus does not have command over. He rules nature and all time, even the Pharisee's sacred sabbath. Jesus further claims that he is the source of divine life. Today's emissaries can operate with the same power by calling upon his Father, Jesus, and the Spirit.

John's portrait of Jesus is one of a cosmic Christ who is preexistent and perfect God. He is eternal life and light. There is no reduction of his power. This is seen in his ability to do miracles, forgive sins, announce himself as Lord of the sabbath, and dwell among us as both God and human flesh. It meshes with the Synoptics' picture of Jesus to present a total life possibility for the believer. In all four Gospels Jesus is both Son of man and Son of God. He is preexistent and seated now at the right hand of the Father. Jesus is both the source of eternal light and the model for dispensing it. He is revered a teacher who is also able to heal. He died but rose again. He was born of a virgin, lived and died as a Jew, but reached out to all persons. There is no greater model for modern missionaries.

ADDENDUM
Paraphrase of John 3:1-16

There was an outstanding Christian television personality who heard Jesus was coming through town and wanted to get him for an interview. He came to see Jesus secretly at night because he was afraid Jesus might say no. Jesus had always seemed to avoid publicity.

When he got to Jesus, he said, "All the folks know you're quite a guy. God is really with you because we've heard you've done a lot of miracles." The room was filled with snow.

Jesus looked straight at him and said, "You've got to come off all flashy gimmicks and be born again."

The television personality said, "How can I be born again? I can't reenter my mother."

Jesus pushed on, "Truly I say to you, you've got to start all over. You can't be on my side unless you do. Right now you're spending 85 percent of the money you take in for production costs. All the while hungry people starve and the elderly are neglected. You know what I mean when I say you've got to start over. The new birth cannot be programmed or captured in a clever symbol. God's work is done wherever people are helped, not entertained."

The television personality asked, "What do you mean?"

Jesus answered, "Are you an internationally renowned expert on religion and you still don't get it? I guess there is no use saying any more. I've been to heaven and back and yet I still know the value of ministry here and now. As Moses gave healing through a snake, one day you may know that the kingdom involves ministry through suffering, not adulation. I give eternal life and you prefer public notoriety.

"God loves his world so very much that he is giving me for your kind. Believe and live! Change and you will know. Stay the same and you have your reward."

8
Luke's Look:
The Holy Spirit Set Loose

Almost all Bible scholars today agree that the physician Luke wrote both the Gospel of Luke and the Acts of the Apostles. The latter is the continuation of the first. Style, vocabulary, and motifs are obviously in common. Therefore, the two may be called Luke-Acts.

Luke-Acts is an opera in which we can detect various themes which emerge again and again. One of these themes is that Luke wants to present an accurate account of how the gospel was spread. He sees himself as the recorder of a supremely significant chain of events. Another basic theme is Luke's desire to clear up any misunderstanding about the relationship between Judaism and Christianity. Luke does this by showing the Jewishness of Jesus. This for Luke demonstrates that Jesus and his disciples did not intend to create a gulf between Jesus and Christians. It was the opposite that was the truth, according to Luke. Luke presents in Acts the new church as the true Israel. Thirdly, Luke wrote to prove that Christianity was no threat to the political authority of the Empire. The mission to the Gentiles is a clear theme in Luke-Acts and is presented as not a political threat.

Three major motifs are characteristic of Lucan writing. One is the roll of the Holy Spirit. There are seventeen references to the Holy Spirit in the Gospel of Luke and fifty-seven in Acts. For Luke, the church is to live in the power of the Spirit until Jesus returns. The second theme is a deep social concern. Any person who stands outside the respected community is given special attention by Luke. Thirdly, Luke gives a special place to women in his writings. Women are highlighted both in Luke and Acts.

The Acts of the apostles is Luke's attempt to preview the missionary work of the early church. It is a handbook par excellence on the subject of missions for all ages. The prayerful missionary will find guidelines themes for almost every experience he will face. The book covers a period of about three decades, from the time of Jesus' ascension until shortly before the death of Paul. Its unmistakable emphasis is on witnessing and extension.

A subtheme of Acts is Jesus' dependence on the Holy Spirit for the success of his mission. Therefore, Acts stresses Jesus' dependence on faithful persons filled with the Holy Spirit. The Holy Spirit is seen as a fulfillment of the promise of the Father. So, for Luke, the gospel of the Spirit completes the gospel of the Son with the help of the missionaries. Thus, Acts is a primer of importance for those who are called to follow in the steps of Jesus, Peter, and Paul and accompanied by the Holy Spirit.

Luke clearly shows in Acts that the most important ministry of the Holy Spirit is in the filling of Christians for service. In Luke's Gospel we see that the lordship of Christ gives the believer authority to bear witness to everyone. The presence of the Holy Spirit gives him the spiritual ability to make an import on those hearing the testimony. Thus, the Spirit accompanied believer never witnesses alone. It is he who makes real the authority and presence of Christ.

Missionaries active in witness and ministy are discovering that the filling of the Spirit is not a nebulous experience which you can only hope to possess. It is a definite, personal, and recognizable experience. The filling of the Spirit is a definite experience to equip God's people for service. It is a commandment of the Bible that the believer is to be filled with the Spirit (Eph. 5:18). This being filled is a continual, repeated action. This filling gives modern witnesses boldness, patience, wisdom, and the ability to witness. The scared and cowering group of disciples in Acts 2 were transformed into a bold and assertive company of witnesses. They discovered that the Holy Spirit is a person who possesses us, instead of a power whom we possess.

For Luke in Acts, the Holy Spirit determines the course of missions as the executor of Christ's will. At least ten times in Acts the Holy Spirit thrusts willing disciples into new fields. For example,

Philip went to the outcast Samaritans. Suddenly, Philip was led to leave the revival among the Samaritans to witness to one man in the Gaza desert. This was Luke's clear demonstration that the Holy Spirit's guidance often conflicts with the logic of man. It is Luke's point that only the Spirit can qualify to determine the place of service for his people. The next move of the Spirit can scarcely be predicted, just obeyed. The one fact that is certain is that faithful disciples are to witness wherever the Holy Spirit has placed them until he directs them to another place. Further, the Holy Spirit periodically speaks through the traditions and the prejudices of his people to thrust them into the world as bold disciples. In that manner the Spirit works through God's people to accomplish his mission. That principle still applies today.

The second book (Acts) in Luke's library begins with a dedication to one Theophilus or "lover of God." He was probably a Gentile, perhaps Roman, who stands as a reminder that Luke is writing to a Gentile audience. It was Luke's intention from the beginning to say that the gospel is applicable to any and all cultures. The Holy Ghost is mentioned in verse 2 as the instigator of Christ's ascension. It is the Spirit who is central actor in the book from the beginning. What Jesus started, the Spirit finishes.

Jesus promises the waiting disciples that they will soon be visited by the Holy Ghost who will empower them from the inside. The stupid disciples still missed the point. They were begging for Jesus to establish the earthly, political kingdom the Israelites had wanted. The Holy Ghost is to come, Jesus reminds them, in order for them to be witnesses. Being empowered by the Spirit is not an end in itself. Those today who enjoy the infilling of the Holy Ghost, but who do not minister as a result, have missed Luke's point in Acts. Rich people who get happy but do not feed the hungry are an embarrassment to the kingdom.

Jesus did leave those early disciples and they went into deep despair. They resorted to the only coping mechanism they could muster at the time, group prayer. (Note "the women" in Acts 1:14, an ever-present help to the disciples in Luke's writings.)

Peter could stand the pressure of waiting no longer. He did what was most natural to him. He started to talk. It was necessary, he maintained, that someone be elected to keep the number of closest disciples at twelve. Matthias was chosen. This set the stage for the greatest single event in church history after the ascension of Christ.

It was fifty days after Passover when the 120 were gathered to pray in a large room. Jerusalem was filled with Jewish celebrants who came to mark this Jewish festival. The disciples were "in one accord"; that is, their hearts and motives were attuned to each other through frantic prayer. No group of missionaries, usually called a mission, have ever come close to being God's messengers to an area without spiritual unity. In the same way, any local church is successful to the degree that the members of the body are "in due accord."

After proper spiritual preparation, the Spirit came, as recorded in Acts 2. The Spirit came with two symbols, sound and sight. Everyone there heard and saw something. There was activity when the Spirit came.

The supernatural gifts which came is often called "speaking in tongues." It was not, however, the same as what was happening in Corinth. At Pentecost one person spoke and everyone understood. At Corinth many spoke at once and no one understood without an interpretation. The Jews from other lands were amazed because they heard the disciples speaking in their own dialects. Most of the audience were Jews from out of Israel. Most responded with appreciation and admiration. Others mocked and accused Peter of being drunk. When the Spirit comes, often the reaction at first is the same as being drunk. But the aftereffects of the fruit of the Spirit are far superior to those of the fruit of the vine. The early church began by being accused of being irreverent but relevant. Today the church is too often very reverent but irrelevant. Today's church is in need of learning that lesson from our brothers nineteen centuries ago. This lesson can only be learned in direct proportion to the freeing reliance on the Holy Spirit.

Peter's sermon in Acts 2:14 and following is a beautiful example of the early church's apologetic method. The first thing we see is that the Old Testament is quoted. Peter felt it necessary to cite scriptural evidence for what he was about to say. He uses Joel as a sign that the last days were upon the world. The surest sign of that was that the Holy Spirit was upon them at that moment. It was Peter's idea that the age to come was here.

Then Peter explains the death of Jesus. He wants the listeners to know that the death of Jesus was no accident. It was the result of a designed plan. The emphasis then shifted to the risen Lord. Jesus died and rose again as the proof of his messiahship. Because he arose, Peter argues, the Holy Spirit is upon him and upon anyone who now wishes to follow Jesus. When the disciples were visited by the Holy Spirit, they were also being visited by the risen Son. This dual dynamite package was to accompany them throughout their generations thrust into the world.

In Acts 2:36, Peter argues that Jesus is God because of his ascension to the Father. This witnessed to Jesus' power over life and death. Only God could have called Jesus to be at his right side. Only Jesus was worthy of that honor. Those gathered at Peter's feet were about to be redistributed through the world in the same power. Jesus, exalted to the right hand of the Father, would oversee the task of Christian missionaries from above.

Peter's argument was quickly comprehended and it gave rise to a quest for guidelines for action. The listeners were ready to act. What should they do now? Peter instantly demanded repentance and baptism. The sermon was highly successful. Three thousand people were baptized and came into the fellowship of the early church. Many of those were Jews from all over the world. Now they must go home and tell the gospel which they had heard and believed. It is quite important to note that these new believers in Christ were instructed in doctrine before they were allowed to go away to witness. Foreign missionaries often deem it necessary for new converts to undergo months of instruction before they are accepted as full church members. The instruction was more than doctrinal. They also grew quickly because they fellowshipped with the apostles. One emphasis aided the other in rapid Christian growth.

Modern missionaries also have much to learn from the life-style of the early Christians as recorded in Acts 2:43-47. At least three of their practices are worthy of present-day emulation. "Wonders and signs" is a word combination Luke uses nine times in Acts. Today pseudosophisticated Christians who believe the age of miracles is past are doing great damage to the church. They have faith only in what can be demonstrated scientifically. Meanwhile, the vast majority of the earth's cultures are given to the mind-set of the "supernatural." God is still working in a miraculous manner through those who are willing to allow him to do so, but only through those.

Secondly, the people held "all things in common." The believers sold all their possessions and contributed the proceeds to a common fund. It was a voluntary action but followed by most. This action was essential to the life of the early Christian community. This provided economic security plus the fact of food for many in the church. Modern cults have given a bad name to this practice because they demand total allegiance symbolized by giving of all belongings to the cult leaders. The Jonestown massacre and the Unification church have both insisted on total giving of possessions. This need not, however, deter voluntary Christian movements from sharing their possessions. Foreign missionaries are discovering that new converts frequently give all they have for survival. This is of necessity for survival at first but it ends up in a quality of life unmatched outside of church. That in itself is a witness.

Thirdly, they were "breaking bread." They shared meals, all of which had a deep religious meaning for the new Christians. The fellowship was of a deep quality and reminiscient of the Last Supper Jesus shared with his disciples.

The result of these three items shared by these early believers was that many were being saved. The number was much greater because the quality was evident. Those faithful witnesses who wish to see the church grow today will do well to evaluate the level of daily sharing shown by the earliest of Christian believers.

Acts 10 is a turning point in Acts. The future of the church depended on its acceptance of Gentiles into the previously all-Jewish fellowship. The gospel, in Luke's eyes, had to be proclaimed to the Gentiles in total disregard of the Jewish rules which would have restricted its spread.

Peter's vision in Acts 10:9-16 signals a breakthrough for the early church. He went up on the roof of Simon the Tanner's house to pray. He was soon asleep. He saw a sheet lowered by the four corners to the earth. In this sheet were all types of unclean animals, reptiles, and birds. A voice spoke commanding him to kill and eat what he saw in the sheet. He was shocked because they were all condemned for a Jew. Twice God had to speak because Peter was so prejudiced about eating such nonkosher items. Peter knew the implications of his vision immediately. In his day, the devout Jew would not even buy oil, bread, milk or meat from a Gentile. To dine in the house of a pagan was an abomination unto the Lord. Gentiles were not to be seen in polite social contacts. Peter was shocked! The Lord, previously known in law, was now calling for Gentiles to be a valid part of the new Israel.

The contingent including Cornelius arrived at the end of the vision. He went down to meet them without delay. The vision was already having its effect on Peter. The irony was that Peter was already being inconsistent by staying in the house of a tanner. According to strict Jewish standards, he was associating himself with one who handled the hides of unclean animals. Peter's eyes were opened because they were already partially opened.

The next day Peter set out for Cornelius' town of Caesarea. Peter was still so upset about his new venture into the Gentile community that he took six witnesses with him, three times the required number. Merely by associating with the people of Cornelius' house, Peter was guilty of a profane act in the eyes of Orthodox Jews. In spite of the risk involved, Peter began to preach. The point of the sermon is that God does not look on the outside of persons. Literally, the Bible says, "does not receive according to the face." This fact has been comprehended often in the church since the days of Peter. The true Israelites are therefore those who "believe on his name." This is the only legitimate distinction of persons in the world today. Persons have worth directly in proportion to their faith response to Jesus of Nazareth. God's grace is for all who believe. Any other standard is beside the point.

Verses 44-48 in Acts 10 serve to remind the reader that the Holy

Spirit comes to Gentiles as well as Jews. Gentiles received the Holy Spirit and the Jews were amazed. Peter rejoiced and asked if anyone would object to the Gentiles being baptized. No one dared fly in the face of the Holy Spirit. But, unfortunately, today they do. Time and space from this event have caused a few narrow Christians to assume that the gospel is only for a few. Our prayer should be that their narrow attitude, as was Peter's sermon, should be interrupted by the Holy Spirit. This was another Pentecost. We need another one to remove the blinders from anyone's eyes who still thinks that God's love is limited.

Acts 15 records that Peter's experience at Cornelius' house did not settle the Gentile issue for good. A whole church council had to be called in Jerusalem to settle the issue. The scene was set when a group of Pharisees came to Antioch posing as legitimate representatives from James, the leader of the church in Jerusalem. They were teaching the new believers in Antioch that they had to follow a series of Jewish rules in order to be true Christians. Paul and Barnabas engaged the Pharisees in debate, arguing that true Christian belief is dependent on faith alone, not on keeping rules. These two were appointed by the church in Antioch to present the problem to the apostles in Jerusalem. Then they provided financial assistance for the trip. This scene shows that clashes in missionary policy always come when some new truth disturbs a group in power. People, Christian and non-Christian alike, get nervous when their traditions are challenged. The ones who respond best are those who are able to "hang loose" in the Spirit instead of being tied to tradition.

The council was convened and the issue of Gentile circumcision was immediately dealt with. Peter was able to give his testimony that God had led him to baptize some uncircumcised Gentiles. But, Peter was still cautious about the whole matter. His argument was a legalistic one, not one that Paul would have used. Peter argued that since the Jews never could keep the law, neither could the Gentiles. Paul would have said more about grace. The result was the same.

James, the half-brother of Jesus, made the final decision. He said, they should not trouble those of the Gentiles who turn to God. He was an early Christian ethics expert who placed the emphasis on marital faithfulness and refraining from idol worship. In other words, the emphasis of the early church was to be on internals, not externals. The keeping of external rules was not as important as witness through faithfulness. All missionaries should remember that lesson when discipling indigenous Christians. It is usually quicker and easier to try to regulate external behavior but long-range success depends on internal growth within the new Christian.

Paul's successful transcultural and interfaith witness in Athens as recorded in Acts 17 is an outstanding model for such work on the modern scene. Athens was a city of about a quarter million and was the intellectual and cultural center of the world. The artists of the city were unsurpassed in literature and other forms of art. Socrates and Plato were famous native sons of Athens. It lay at the commercial crossroads of the Greek and Roman world. In Paul's day the city had the best university of the Western world. It was a democratic city-state with the authority vested in the Areopagus, the city's judicial council. Athens was very similar to the cities of New Orleans or New York in America today.

Paul was waiting for two of his missionary colleagues to return from Berea. Instead of spending his time buying souvenirs or sightseeing, Paul thought immediately of taking the gospel of Christ to the people where they were. The synagogue and the public markets were Paul's pulpits as he took the risen Lord to the people. Paul could not sit still in a situation where the signs of idolatry were so rampant. The "market place" was a gathering place for all Athenians who wanted to listen to the latest philosophy. Speaker after speaker would mount his soapbox as in Hyde Park in London. "Those who chanced to be there were there for a purpose; that is, to hear the latest.

On a regular basis two types of philosophy were represented there. The first was the Stoic. It was founded by one Zeno in the fourth century BC, in Athens. It was better known in this city than anywhere else in the world. They taught that the logos (reason or logic) created the universe. (It was against this background that John wrote the prologue to his Gospel.) They also taught that the laws of nature must be followed in order to attain integrity or virtue. One was to "go with the flow" of the natural order without doing anything to disturb it. The Stoics thought that there exists a giant "soul bank." In each person, Zeno maintained, there is a spark of the logos and at death this divine spark returns back to this giant "soul bank." The Stoic view of life taught the immortality of the soul.

In the 1970s Americans spent a quarter billion dollars on religions telling them to "be cool" and "go with the flow." Transcendental meditation alone accounted for half this amount. Persons still flock to promises of inner peace built on their own inner resources. Stoicism is far from dead. According to a Gallup Poll on religion taken in 1979, 28 percent of adult Americans say they believe in reincarnation as a way of explaining life after death. The idea of the "soul bank" is growing. Stoicism is still a force to be reckoned with by articulate Christians.

The Epicureans represented a school founded by Epicurus in the fourth century BC. They taught that the gods were concerned with the affairs of the human family. They taught that at death each one simply returns to atoms. There is no survival after death. Ethically, they advocated avoiding pain rather than seeking pleasure. The Epicureans were quite passive rather than the pleasure-seekers as they are often stereotyped.

When Paul stepped into the open marketplace, the philosophers called him names. Their favorite was "seed picker." This was to say that Paul was intellectually a scavenger who merely picked up bits of information and spread them without using any discernment. Today the apologist for the Christian faith can expect to be harassed by those who disagree. He will not escape attack by those most affected by his teachings. The philosophers knew they had much to lose if Paul's view of Jesus' resurrection were correct. They also called Paul "one who set forth foreign deities." They heard him to be only another outsider with some theory about a dying and rising god. Paul withstood the attacks.

The philosophers gave up trying to embarrass Paul and whisked him off to the city council for a hearing. This council could still judge in matters pertaining to murder and religion, in spite of ruling

Roman authority. The assembly possessed the right also to assign and authorize public lecturers. Perhaps the pagan philosophers wanted to keep Paul from speaking in public again. The council decided they wanted to hear Paul before they judged the matter.

Paul stood up to speak. All eyes were glued on him. He started by saying they were overly concerned about demons. That has certainly been the case in American religion in the 1970s. Demons rose to the fore in credence among the general public in the decade preceding 1980. Exorcisms were popularized in a decade given to destiny with the devil. Belief in a personal Satan almost doubled while belief in God declined slightly, according to a 1979 Gallup Poll on religion.

Some groups place too much emphasis on demons. They see demons in every corner of every sanctuary. They see multiple demons in every believer. Exorcisms become painful and costly while poorly trained exorcists move from church to church offering their services. This is not to deny the current existence of demons even in sophisticated societies, however. The question is the degree to which one becomes obsessed with finding demons in too many places. Many modern missionaries are finding natives of animistic nations to be open to the gospel in direct proportion to the missionary's ability to demonstrate Christ's power over evil spirits. The audiences become receptive when their dominant world view is accepted.

Acts 17, verse 22 may also be translated "religious." That fact is universally true. Not only in ancient Athens can it be said that persons are religious. More than three thousand new religions were begun in the 1970s in America alone. Persons will worship, whether it be a Thunderbird on top of a totem pole on an Indian reservation or one in a new-car showroom. That Greek word may also be translated "superstitions." Even sophisticated modern Americans are openly superstitions, even though most cannot openly admit it. There is prevalent here, for example, a paranoia about trisdadekaphobia, or fear of the number 13. Multi-million dollar commercial aircraft have no row 13. Multi-billion dollar hotels and office complexes have no floor 13. Most of us are like a woman in Las Vegas who said, "I don't believe in ghosts, I'm just scared of them." Decisions are made in order to avoid offending anyone who believes in superstition. The mythical "African nature" is no more superstitious than most Americans.

The people were so religious that they had erected an altar with the inscription, "To the Unknown God." This was probably done to be certain that none of the gods were not left out and thereby offended. This inscription Paul took as his text. They had a god who was unknown. He knew one personally because of his contact with the risen Lord. It was Paul's thesis that the people of Athens were already worshiping the one true God but were ignorant of him personally. Paul presented Almighty God as the one and only Creator of the universe. This fact alone he hoped would expose the folly of their idol worship. The very one who had made the materials which made the idols was among them yet unrecognized. At this busy crossroads city, Paul also argued that the very one who created all nations and peoples was the one he represented. Paul was using the most valid of all transcultural witnessing techniques. He took the people where he found them and went from there. Paul also spoke a great universal truth when he said that people grope in darkness while ignorantly searching for the one true God. The gospel is the good news that God reaches down in Christ to find the groper. It could be said that the entire world outside of Christ is involved in "gospel groping."

Paul continues his mission sermon by quoting from the known wisdom of the hometown Stoic philosophers. Thus he continued his excellent method of relating to truths the people already had. He did not condemn them for what they already knew, Paul simply wanted to lead them one step closer to God. The phrase, "In him we live and move and have our being" is part of a poem written by the famous Epimenides, a poet of sixth century BC, Greece. The phrase "for we are indeed his offspring" comes from Aratus a fourth-century BC sage from Tarsus. The salient point Paul is making is that since their own favorite poets argue that all persons depend on God, for their being, why should they argue the point? Paul had done his homework. He knew almost as much about Stoic philosophy as any man or woman in Athens. No one there could say that he was witnessing from a vacuum to a vacuum. Paul's sources were reliable. The listeners were then thinking that perhaps Paul's message was just as reliable. The modern missionary can afford to pay no less a price today in learning about the culture he is trying to penetrate with the gospel. This learning must occur both before and during the emissary's life among his chosen people.

Paul's next point is one he drives home in the first three chapters of Romans; that is, up till now God has allowed persons the right to find him through nature or the law. But, humans themselves were not able to find God through nature or the law on their own. God saw that in times prior to Christ, so he offered a perfectly clear revelation in the risen Lord. Because that revelation is now so clear, God's patience wears thin with those who cannot see him now. Now he demands repentance. The proof of that clear revelation is the risen Christ, who serves as a symbol of hope for those who believe. For those who refuse to believe in the light of all this evidence, their fate is one of living under God's negative judgment.

The sermon ends abruptly. This was probably due to the fact that Paul was rudely interrupted by some who poked fun at the very idea of a Nazarene carpenter being able to rise from the dead. To most of the listeners there, the idea was absurd, since they believed that no one exists after death except in an atom form. A few said they would be willing to hear Paul again sometime. Some people did believe, including one of the influential city council members. It is difficult to tell how great his influence may have been in the next generation. Church tradition indeed states that Dionysius became the first bishop of Athens. It should also be remembered that a woman named Damaris believed. Paul was overjoyed to think of her possible influence among those females not deemed worthy of discussing philosophical concepts at the city council.

Paul's stay in Athens was anything but a failure. It was a success not only because of those who believed but also because of those who wanted to hear more. Paul was planting, others would water. The greatest of the early church's missionaries and evangelists understood that the results were not up to him. Further, he under-

stood that not everyone would believe the gospel. Veteran missionaries today testify that it took them decades to learn those two lessons. The sooner they are learned today the quicker they can be
applied. The sooner they are applied, the more relaxed and effective will be the witness.

Acts 19:11-19 serves as a humorous reminder to all who would
be missionaries in the future. The point is that no one can go out to
do God's will flippantly. There were, it seems, seven sons of a
Jewish high priest who were itinerant exorcists. Sceva was not a
recognized priest so he may have been one who allowed his sons to
try magic to gain a name for themselves. These shallow sons had
seen Paul do miracles in Ephesus through the power of Jesus. They
decided to try the same thing even though they probably were not
Christian believers. They made another mistake in that they chose
to try to deal with a demon-possessed man, a task difficult enough
for prayed-up Christians. The sons were shocked when the formula
boomeranged on them. They fled naked and wounded because
they underestimated the power of Satan and overestimated the
power of the formula.

Note that God made the most of a bad situation. The news
spread quickly and the people saw clearly that the real spiritual
power lay in Jesus, not in his disciples or some special formula.
Some of the new Christians were practicing magic on the sly. When
they saw and heard what happened to the sons of Sceva, they gave
up their magical crafts. They saw how truly dangerous it can be to
play around with demons and the black arts. They brought all their
books and burned them publicly. The 50,000 pieces of silver represented the modern equivalent of $15,000, a great amount. The
"books" were probably composed of lists of magic formulas. If the
strong names of Jesus and Paul were not powerful enough to stop
demons, the other formulas were impotent and too dangerous to
play with. Even the name of Jesus has no magic within itself.

Most of the world today is peopled by persons who believed in
evil spirits. If missionaries enter into these territories flippantly or ill-
prepared, they are doomed to failure. God still does not allow be-

lievers or nonbelievers to take his name in vain; that is, treat it lightly. There are no automatic formulas when dealing with the personal evil in today's world. This drives today's witness to rely solely on the Lord. The Holy Spirit works only with those open to him and him only.

Luke's account of the spread of the gospel in his missionary manual called Acts, ends with Paul in Rome. The apostle's lifelong dream had finally come true. Paul was, after all, a Roman citizen. His love for the city was hardly dampened by the fact that he came to the city as a prisoner. As soon as he got to the city he consulted with the Jewish leaders. There was never any dampening of Paul's desire to spread the gospel in spite of his conditions. Paul's persistence is an object lesson to all who would overcome obstacles to the gospel. Paul's love and hope he had found in the gospel was strong enough to go beyond temporary imprisonment.

Paul knew how to use every situation. He persuaded many of the Jews who heard him to hear him again at his lodging. On that second occasion he took all day to show the skeptical Jewish leaders how the law was fulfilled in Jesus. Paul was wise enough not to try to do it all at once in terms of witnessing. He could bide his time when necessary. When the majority of the Jews in Rome refused to believe, Paul still took refuge in the fact that the church of the future would be composed of Gentiles.

Acts 28:30-31 is Luke's summary statement to conclude the book. He states that Paul had full freedom in preaching the gospel. This ends the greatest missionary manual in the history of the church. Luke had shown us what a small group of bold believers can do when turned loose in the Spirit on the world. This small group saw the Spirit leap over social, religious, and political barriers. The gospel would not be bound. It was for the Jewish and Gentile worlds. Today the gospel is proven daily to be universally applicable to human need. The gospel today as yesterday, shines whenever loving people take it to persons prepared by the Holy Spirit. The connection comes when faith melts the faithful as in the missionary manual called Acts.

ADDENDUM
Paraphrase of Acts 17:16-34

Paul's missionary friends left him alone in Atlanta while they went to Chattanooga and Augusta. While Paul had a few days alone, he was made sick to his stomach by the warped ethical values he saw in Atlanta.

So, he went immediately to the central business district and began to dialogue with anyone who was there and was willing.

Then the people who wanted nothing but to have a good time on the disco scene were joined by the TM lecturers and they challenged Paul. Bystanders were heard to say, "What is this weird out-of-town dude going to say next?" They thought he was crazy because Paul preached succinctly unto them the fact that Jesus had risen physically from his grave.

So they took him and brought him to Major Jackson's chambers, saying, "Tell us more of this new and different idea of yours. We want to hear because your ideas are so strange to us. What does all this mean?"

(All the folks in Atlanta spent most of their time spreading gossip and rumors.)

Then Paul stood before the city council and said, "You people of Atlanta, I have seen that in all things you are very religious. I have seen it myself. Your statues and rituals are too many to count. In fact, you even have one labeled "To the Unknown God" just so you won't leave any god out. It is my pleasure to tell you that the one you are groping in the dark for is right here among us. The true God made everything in existence. Since he is the ruler of earth and all surrounding galaxies he cannot be contained in any fancy statues. Also, he cannot be represented by any human art. He is totally self-sufficient. It is he who gives all of us our very next breath and even life's basic necessities.

This one true God who raised Jesus has made us all originally to be brothers and sisters in the human family. He has created all natural order. Those who can see this order should continue to grope after him because he has been here all the while. In God we have life itself. Even some of your Southern writers have said, "We are God's dear children."

Since we are all God's children, it is evident that God cannot be captured by any kind of earthly building material. God has been pretty patient up to now but he's through playing around right now. You had better repent and quit playing games with him. This is true because there's a great day coming in which God will judge all of us by the standards of the risen Lord.

When the city council members heard of Jesus' resurrection, most laughed. A few said, "Someday, Paul, we'd like to hear some more about this Jesus of yours." So Paul left. A few important people got saved that day in Atlanta, including a city council member named Ralph and a woman named Susan and some others.

9
Paul's Pens:
The Hope of Glory

The apostle Paul is without a doubt the brightest personality of the first-century Christian church (excluding Jesus, of course). He was at once the greatest missionary, evangelist, and theologian of the early church. He understood that one does not have to sacrifice any of those three emphases to be successful in one or two of the others. Paul understood and demonstrated that the mind, the will and the feet can all be equally dedicated to the glory of God because of that balance; no person of the apostolic age labored more successfully for the gospel.

Born with the name Saul and later called Paul, this man was of the tribe of Benjamin. He was born in Tarsus of Cilicia. He was taught the trade of tentmaking from the early age. It is obvious that he had an affluent father, a Roman citizen and a Jew, who saw to it that his son Saul received a good education. He studied under the greatest rabbi of his day, Gamaliel of Jerusalem. The subject was rabbinical theology. Paul was versed in the pharisaical law, as shown by his writing method and vocabulary. Through it all, Paul developed a great personality charged with zeal, courage, and emotion. That zeal was first directed to the defense of God's law, in the tradition of the Pharisees.

During this early period, Paul saw the new Christian religion as a great threat to truth. The Jewish leaders in Jerusalem saw in him a great tool for exterminating the new believers. This they did to the degree that they sent him to Damascus of Syria to kill the Christians there. On the road to Damascus, as Paul tells it, he became an eyewitness to the risen Christ. In one event he was saved and called to be an apostle to the Gentiles. Paul set the pattern for all Christians. In the truest sense, all believers are emissaries. There is no way that a mere believer can escape his delightful responsibility of witnessing for Christ. The call to be a Christian is within itself a call to make disciples. Mission boards will continue to appoint full-time professional missionaries but this fact does not lessen the necessity of all being missionaries in the name of Jesus.

Paul wasted no time getting his missionary career going. He proclaimed in the synagogue of Damascus the truth that "this Jesus is the Son of God." But Paul soon discovered that he was not completely ready for the task. Never again would he walk into a situation unprepared. So he retired for three years to Arabia for a period of prayer and preparation. Today it often seems harsh for a mission board to require two years of experience and a year of language school before allowing a missionary candidate to go to his chosen field. There is biblical precedent for this procedure, however. Paul was never again to be accused of being unprepared spiritually or intellectually.

After his first missionary journey to Antioch, Judea, Cyprus, Perga, South Galatia, Iconium, Lystra, and Derbe, Paul won a basic battle at the council in Jerusalem in AD 49. Paul was able to convince James and other church leaders that if Gentiles were forced to be circumcised in order to be Jewish Christians, then the gospel was secondary and not primary. The risk of Christianity being a forgettable sect of Judaism was averted.

The second missionary journey of Paul included most of the stops on the first journey plus Troas, Philippi, Ephesus, Thessalonica, Berea, Athens, Corinth, and again Jerusalem.

The third missionary journey was one spent trying to undo the harm done by the Judaizers, who tried to convince Paul's converts that one must obey the law to be a Christian. He visited Galatia again, Phrygia, Ephesus, Macedonia, Illyricum, Corinth, Philippi, Troas, and Caesarea. From there he was taken to Rome where he was imprisoned, released, and later died.

Paul's life was one of verbal witness, and fortunately for other believers in later times, also a period of writing. The apostle Paul wrote almost half of the New Testament (13 of the 27 letters). Four times he wrote to individual journeying Christians and nine times to struggling churches. They are all basically letters of an absent missionary to new Christians. These letters of Paul are highly personal documents. He writes with passion to those trying to etch out a Christian identity in the midst of a pagan world. He knows the future of the church is up for grabs. Paul was such a successful missionary that his mission field soon grew too large for him to handle with personal visits. He had to write with feeling to try to encourage and instruct new believers and pastors in order to preserve the fruits of his work. Paul's letters often reflect the intensity with which he took his task as missionary.

Paul was a pioneer in religious thought, opening a way for the truth of the gospel to the Gentile world. He wrote with passion to grow these people who had no frame of reference for being believers. To grow them in the Lord, Paul used passion, logic, sentiment, and strong argument. These are wired with tenderness and strength intermingled. Paul used all the weapons he could muster to win and keep the allegiance of these baby Christians. It was fortunate that Paul knew Greek from his childhood. His mind was fertile and flexible in expression.

Paul's work as apostle to the Gentiles and church planter was exposed to three chief assaults, all three of them which have modern counterparts. The first attack was from the Jewish Christians of legalistic mindset who wanted all Christians to follow the law of Moses. There are still those who view the Christian life as following a set of rules. Put them in a different culture with the gospel message and then try to get everyone to follow the rules. They dress everyone up to suit themselves and get everyone who is a new convert to follow the rigid rules to God. All the while they have missed the point of the gospel; that is, freedom in faith. The second assault came from the pagan idolatry of the Gentile peoples with which the new converts were surrounded. There is not a missionary in the world who does not struggle to help his converts know the difference between gospel behavior and the standards of the secular world. The third assault to the early gospel was that of the gnostic heresy. This idea denied that Jesus had an earthly body since flesh is evil. The incarnation of Jesus was said to be impossible since God remains removed from the world. All these ideas went against Paul's assertion that Jesus was really man and really God.

Paul wrote primarily to speak to individual situations which arose between his visits to the churches he planted. In spite of the occasional nature of most of his letter, Paul did present through it all a systematic plan of his thoughts. He repeated those themes which meant most to him. They included five, all of which have present-day application to the doing of missions.

First, Paul stressed the kingdom of God. For Paul, the church in all ages consists of the citizens of God's kingdom (Phil. 3:20). Christ is the unifying principle of God's reign on earth which embraces all of reality, including the sacred and secular aspects of life. In Paul's letters, the throne of God's kingdom is the heart and it is empowered through the Holy Spirit. In the end, the kingdom will liberate all of nature plus the children of God. The kingdom is opposed by a dominion of darkness but this domination will one day be eternally and powerfully overthrown.

This concept of the kingdom is applicable to modern missions. The evil kingdom is at work in the hearts of those outside the gospel. These persons are ready to fight the gospel carriers at the drop of a gospel tract. The missionary is realistic only when he recognizes this fact of spiritual warfare.

The second major theme for Paul is the church. Paul understood well that Christian salvation is just as social as personal. The church was no mere temporal institution for Paul. She was presented as one day appearing in all her splendor at the feet of Jesus. The church is held together by the grave of Christ and is the means through which one exercises his gifts along with other believers. When God's grace gifts are exercised, the church is headed toward fullness. Today's most effective missionaries are those who grant new converts the right to recognize and exercise their gifts in the church. There is little room for dictatorships in the mission field. The body is built up for a bright future through all her members.

The third major Pauline theme is "new life" in Christ. It is notable that all believers in Christ are saints to Paul. In fact, the word *saint* appears nowhere in the Bible in the singular. New persons in Jesus

Christ, according to Paul, can transform all earthly events and relations. Even the basic obligations to the family and state are not removed but heightened and deepened by allegiance to Christ (Rom. 13:1-3). Basic activities such as eating and drinking are even done to the glory of God (Col. 3:17). Paul was not simply doing theology when he wrote such truths. He was "in Christ" (Gal. 2:20). Paul, as master missionary, foreknew that total redemption is the only kind that is any good on mission fields. No partial gospel can last very long anywhere it is being challenged constantly. This truth allows the active missionary to know that the gospel is applicable anywhere it goes.

Paul also had a grasp on the major role of sin in the human family. He taught that all have sinned as a past fact. No one can deny or escape that truth. This universal sin affects all peoples, even those carefully chosen to be God's special children. This sin manages to accumulate in a culture and in the whole human race. As a result, God's wrath is resident on and in all of us. Even the law of Moses brought no long range help to Jews because it was impossible to keep. But, Christ comes to institute a new age, one which makes rule-keeping necessary (Gal. 3:13).

So today, all persons regardless of cultural background, must exercise their own faith to escape God's wrath. For Paul, faith is the trusting act in which the sinner meets God's outstretched hand filled with forgiveness. The salvation which results is one which includes the individual's total being, both soul and body. Paul had no patience with just "soul-winning" or any other cheap-grace evangelism which implies that God is only interested in one aspect of a person's being (2 Cor. 6:20). The resurrection of Jesus seals salvation for the sinner. Through faith it can become a settled reality.

This full gospel message is an effective one in modern missions. Medical, agricultural, and educational missions can bring persons to Christ because they demonstrate that God loves all of us. This is also a part of the gospel package which insists that all persons are living in sin unless they exercise faith in the living Christ.

The fifth and final theme in Paul's theology of mission is his emphasis on the identity of the true God. He begins by saying, "To us there is but one God, the Father, of whom are all things, and we in him" (1 Cor. 8:6). God the Father is accompanied presently by God the Son. The fact that Christ is Lord does not reduce God as Father but proves the unity of the Godhead. This is also true of the divinity of the Holy Spirit (2 Cor. 13:14). The Holy Spirit is God dwelling in the individual believer and the church. There are times today on the mission field when each of the three aspects of the Godhead can communicate across language and cultural ones. To some peoples, God as Father and the one true God is the message to which they respond most readily. Some push to the message that God's Spirit is present and available to all listeners. Most respond favorably to the idea of a mediator who comes to them with forgiveness. The Godhead in all three facets is easily understood by all peoples in the world. Paul as master missionary understood and taught this truth.

There are five sections of Paul's theology which deserve special attention for modern missionary thought and action. The first is the entire section of Romans 9—11. Here Paul speaks to the issue of the Jews. He begins by expressing his sorrow that the Jews have not responded en masse to the person of Christ. At times Paul had to argue that one does not have to be Jewish to be Christian. Now he grieves that most Jews are not Christians. Today half the world's Jews live in the United States. The numbers are fourteen million in the world and seven million in America. In 1981 there are more Jews in Miami or Chicago than in Jerusalem. There are more Jews in the New York City area than in the entire state of Israel. Today the American Christian community is split over whether to bear an evangelical witness to the seven million Jews here. The Liberal Protestant community and most Roman Catholics view the Jews as God's chosen people even in this day. Therefore they conclude that Jews should not be targets of witness. To call them "lost" is to insult them as not being God's special people today; the argument goes. To "convert" Jews, some Jewish leaders argue, is to do a time reversal back to Nazi persecution when forced conversion was the order of the day. Most Christians in the American nations do not consider modern Jews as legitimate targets of evangelism. Most evangelical Christians, on the other hand, contend that they have the right and commission to witness of the "born again" experience to their Jewish friends. Romans 9:1-3 certainly stands on their side.

Paul expresses his anguish over the Jew's refusal to believe. This is strongly seen in Paul's declaration that he would gladly surrender his own salvation in exchange for that of his Jewish brethren. No greater concern can be expressed by a born-again Christian. A prayer this deep comes only out of concerned love.

Now Paul lists six advantages of the Jewish people. These six read as a review of Old Testament history and theology. The first is sonship, a title of witnessing which only the Father can grant (Hos. 11:1). The second is glory, or the vital center of Jewish worship. Paul had found this same glory in the face of Jesus (2 Cor. 3:18). He wants his Jewish neighbors to discover that same presence. Thirdly, Paul mentions the covenants. These within themselves show God's love for his people. He continues to desire a relationship with the people he chose. In the fourth place, Paul lists the law. It was this which should have led the Jews to God, but they could not obey it. In fifth place Paul listed the personal example set by the patriarchs such as Abraham. Finally, there are the promises reaching back to the time of Abraham (Isa. 55:3). This section concludes with the mention of Christ, sent to replace all six mentioned by Paul.

In Romans 9:6-13, Paul argues four points. God never gives up on a covenant. His promises never fail. To argue that the covenant has been cancelled is not to say anything negative about God. Since the Jews have been unfaithful, Christ is now the fulfillment of all the ancient promises. Today most of Israel has rejected Christ. But, the faithful should not give up because God will preserve a faithful remnant of believers who relate to Christ in faith. As God chose Jacob over Esau, He now prefers the faithful Christians to the unfaithful Jews.

In the rest of chapter 9, Paul speaks of God's freedom to elect as he chooses. This doctrine shows that God, in his soverignty, has chosen a new Israel. To argue with that point is to argue with God's Word and right to choose one people over another. Christ was a stumbling block to the hardhearted Jews of Paul's day but a blessing to those who had faith. The once-hated Gentiles are now those through whom God displays his love most clearly. Paul argues that God can use anyone, Egyptians or Gentiles. The method is to shock Israel back into vital belief.

Chapter 10 is an elevation of Christ in the midst of this statement about Israel. There is much of an autobiographical element here. Paul formerly had much zeal but that zeal for persecuting Christians was done out of ignorance. It was before he knew the Lord. Paul knew that zeal without knowledge is fanaticism and that zeal with knowledge is genuine enthusiasm. The two are as badly confused today as they were in Jewish legalism. Then Paul makes a point; that is, persons tend to increase zeal when they are wrong. The final point is that false zeal is ended when Christ comes. Zeal is sealed when faith in Christ comes. Faith replaces the law when the Lord comes. It is based on the historical event of the death and resurrection of Jesus. Righteousness comes when confession of faith is made. It is a universal offer. In the faith which Christ makes possible, there are no disappointments or exceptions. Paul was stressing that there is only one way of salvation for both Jews and Gentiles.

Today, as always, the human family seeks for the place it so desperately needs outside of Christ. All the while, mere confession of faith in Jesus will suffice for the blending of all races and cultures. So today all peoples are as responsible for not having forgiveness as Israel is. Israel heard the gospel but did not believe. Israel is responsible for her own failure to find God's righteousness. Today God still allows persons from any culture to go to hell. This he does because he wants human beings to remain free at any cost. God does not send anyone to eternal punishment but is perfectly willing to allow any human to choose that for himself.

Romans 11 completes this section by emphasizing the concept of the remnant. Here Paul argues that God has not rejected the true Israel but only the unfaithful. Paul's proof is personal. "I myself am an Israelite." Paul in no way feels rejected, even though he is a part of Israel. Jews, God has not automatically rejected all of Israel. In verses 7-10 Paul makes it clear that Israel as a whole failed to hold on to the promise which God gave them. As Israel was existent in

God's love, the people were unaware of a future catastrophe growing out of her rejection of Jesus. Israel—past, present, and future— was unaware of her feeling of security which was taking her on the road to ruin. Israel nevertheless continued to confuse her call with blessing, not responsibility as people of faith.

In Romans 11:11-12 is a succinct restatement of the entire three chapters. The Gentiles have been called to be God's new Israel to make the original chosen people jealous and call them back to repentance. Israel did not stumble just so God could make her fall. In God's plan, God will reach Israel in the future through the Gentiles. Paul saw himself as then preaching to the Gentiles in order to do Israel a favor. Israel will one day return to her chosen and responsible position as God's people through the evangelistic faith of the hated Gentiles. Thus, Israel's rejection is but a temporary setback. Now Israel's number of faithful is being cut down so that she can be made full one day. This caused Paul to speed up his apostolic ministry to the Gentiles in order to make Israel see what she was missing. The only factor that is missing is the renewed faith of Israel.

In the allegory of the olive tree, found in Romans 11:17-24, the Gentiles are warned to keep their humility. The Gentiles are receivers and not givers. What they were feeling in Rome could develop into anti-Semitism. This whole attitude has been a blight on the church. Martin Luther argued that Jews should live in ghettoes and/or be run from Germany. Before him, the Catholic rulers of Spain expelled the Jews from that nation in 1492. In the 1940s, Hitler was alive to preach anti-Semitism and succeed in eliminating six million Jews. Today one can hear in churches the spoken idea that all Jews are rich and crooked in business. That hangover is keeping Gentile Christians today (the majority) from being effective as witnesses to their Jewish friends. The even greater harm is done in dehumanizing the Jewish people who have historically been forced to death or expulsion from nations. Gentile Christians need to be reminded even today that we are grafted by grace into the true trunk of the tree of Israel. Even when Gentiles are called the "new people of God," this title does not keep them from regarding

Israel as the orignial people of God. There is a sense in which Israel is still God's people. The only hope or standing either of them has is faith. When this faith is displayed by either people, God is waiting eagerly to pour out his mercy and goodness.

The section in Romans 11:25-36 closes this whole speech by Paul. The closing argument is that Gentiles who do not grant Israel a special place currently are guilty of conceit. The Jews will one day be grafted back into the true trunk of God's faithing people. Paul then concludes that all of Israel and even the Gentiles will be saved, at least those willing to exercise faith. God will love Israel into reconciliation for the sake of faithful patriarchs like Abraham. This future redemption will come as a result of God's mercy, not the merit of Jews in keeping the law. This is based on God's riches (Col. 1:27). Thus, the section closes with a doxology to a loving God who loves all who respond in faith to him.

These three chapters are a reminder to modern missionaries that God is zealous that all people everywhere come to know him through faith in Christ. If God was willing to graft the faithless Gentiles into the trunk of Israel, then he desires all to come to him. Any missionary who views himself as morally better than another out of his own merit is condemning himself. There is no room for pride in the Christian faith, nor any room for an over/under view of the national converts.

First Corinthians 3:11 is the verse on which the whole book's title is built. In this verse Paul argues that the one foundation of the church is Jesus Christ and his gospel. No ultimate philosophy apart from Christ will work on the mission field. He is the only immoveable foundation for mission service. He is the only basis for the creation and continuation of the church, wherever it is found.

Galatians 2:20-21 offers Paul's own testimony in having seen the law crucified to faith. Death to law meant that it ceased to have any further claim on him. The point is clear: keeping the law can keep a faithful believer from following God. "With Christ I stand crucified" is Paul's powerfully dramatic statement. Paul identified with Christ and his death on the cross. This did not diminish his life, but added to it. There is no masochism here. When Paul identified with Christ,

Christ returned the favor. The next verse sums up the entire preceding passage. Anyone who lives by the law tends to diminish the role of grace. The gospel is in jeopardy anywhere the law rules. Religious legalism of any kind renders meaningless the death of Christ. Christ died for nothing if his followers continue to follow the law. The gospel of grace will win in any individual's life when the law is forgotten, and directly in proportion to the way this is done.

The problem in Galatia is exactly the same which plagues most evangelical churches today. Saved by grace, the new believer is then handed a list of rules indicating what he will not do to glorify Christ. The exact list varies but the phenomenon is the same. The new Christian walks away from his first month of Christian discipling by concluding that God saves by grace but keeps through law. That fault is easy to see in others, such as Seventh-Day Adventists. The joy and assurance of salvation is lost by their emphasis on keeping dietary and Sabbath laws. Evangelical Christians, however, often fail to see the same error in our own systems. Law takes the spontaneity out of Christian discipleship. It reduces what started as a relationship to what ends up as resentful rule-following.

The problem at Galatia was that Peter was cavorting with the Gentiles until the rule-keeping Judaizers came near. Then he claimed that he had had nothing to do with those unclean people. The keeping of laws invariably makes hypocrites out of believers. Building a relationship with the Christ, however, brings growth in grace. Let all missionaries beware who still feel that the best way to Christianize new Christians is to force them to obey a set of rules. Under those conditions, a relationship to Christ develops slowly if at all.

Philippians 4:10-13 constitutes a grateful response from Paul for the gifts Paul received from the church at Philippi. Here he expressed gratitude for their generous gifts. But, he reminds them that his true resources are within his own person. They are there because Christ lives in him, not out of his own energies. The strength he has found in Christ is so vital that he can live in whatever condition he finds himself. Paul knew the extremes of abundance and abasement. At times he was almost glorified by the new believers.

At other times his own life was in jeopardy because he preached Jesus' gospel without fear. Paul was saying that he had learned to live with praise as well as criticism.

Paul learned early in his ministry that if he gave the praise he received to Christ, he could also give the criticism. The word Paul uses for "content" is the Greek word for "autocrat." Paul's inner strength is from within and not dependent on externals around him. Yet, Paul's strength was not within himself naturally. It came only as a result of Christ's strength flowing through him. Paul learned this lesson only through experience. Note that Paul was no monk or guru living on a mountaintop. He took the gospel to the market-place. While he enjoyed the gift sent to him by the Philippians, he could have done just as well without it. His true strength was what he wanted for the Philippians; dependency on Christ. He understood that outward circumstances could change but found inner fulfillment through reliance on Christ.

Modern missionaries learn this same lesson either early or late. Praise and promises from persons can vanish quickly in the midst of trying missionary service. Opposition comes thick and fast at times. Only Christ can compensate in such times. The inner strength is there in spite of changing circumstances. Response to the gospel is due to Christ's credit. The missionary is but an instrument as grace flows through him because it resides in him.

The prologue to Paul's letter to the Colossians is a high moment in New Testament Christology. Here Christ is set forth in a cosmic contest. It is clear that Christ is more than one who died on a cross. Christ will simply not be put in a minor place in world history. The dominant heresy Paul fought in the prologue was that of gnosticism. These philosophers despised all common people as being incapable of a reasonable faith. They also denied that Jesus was in human flesh because flesh was evil.

After a brief greeting, Paul launched into a beautiful statement about the whole world's dependency on Christ. The whole letter is given to the unique dignity resident in Christ. The gospel of Christ, according to Paul, is capable of growing because it has power within itself. This power allows each believer, not just the elite, the ability to increase in God's knowledge. All of these may be summed up in the word *redemption*. So, Paul's readers had great reason to rejoice. This is one of the greatest prayers in the Bible.

Paul expounds the fullness of Christ in Colossians 1:15-23. For Paul, Christ is unmatched in his ability to bring humans to God. He is the unique Son of God in whom God's character is reproduced perfectly. If anyone would see God, he should look at Jesus of Nazareth. As such, Jesus is number one in God's heart. Christ is without rival in bringing man to God and God to man. Christ is the only revelation of God which can apply today to all races and cultures. But, Paul's Christ is more than a personal Redeemer.

Christ is number one in God's eyes in the whole universe. He is from eternity to eternity. It is he who created everything that is. Christ was the agent through whom all things came to be. Further, Christ is the goal, as well as the origin, of all that is or has been.

Christ, according to Paul, may be called the "Elmer's Glue" of the universe. Paul says that "in him all things stand together." Christ gives unity and order to the universe. He holds the feathers on the birds and the fenders on the automobile. Ours is the Christ who was God's agent in creation, who stands both behind and ahead of the entire universe. It is Christ who gives coherence to the universe. It is he who, across cultural lines, makes all things new and meaningful.

The modern missionary does not represent a second-rate Messiah figure who died in an ignoble manner. He is the very one who made and remakes all of life itself. He can be carried without embarrassment into any kingly throne room or bushtown in the world.

Colossians 1:27 points out that all of this is possible because Christ can live in us today. This fact affords hope to all of us. This is the glory which God originally intended for all the human race, but sin wrecked the plan. The result is that God's presence resided in us. God's glory is ours. Thus, the present-day emissary is representing a cosmic Christ who is holding the entire universe together today. This gives hope to the missionary and potential hope to all who will believe.

Paul, as missionary and thinker, was the almost perfect model for modern missions. He was not Christ but he knew the secret of having Christ flowing in and through him. This gave him such hope that he could not keep it a secret. May his type increase.

ADDENDUM
Paraphrase of Colossians 1:1-17

I, Paul, an arrow shot by the bow of God, and our dear brother, Timothy; to the faithful ones in Christ who happen to dwell in Colossae; may God pour out his loving presence on you. May you also know the amazing and comforting presence of Christ. Timothy and I are constantly praising the name of God for your deep faith and active love in pursuit of other Christians. We are also very thankful for the hope laid up for you in heaven. This hope is yours only because of the truth inherent in the gospel today.

Your active love in Christ is so remarkable that even Epaphras had told us of it. So we pray for you daily that your strong faith may become even stronger. We are praying that your faith will be strengthened by an even deeper wisdom of the things of God. This we know to be possible because the power of God is available to you. When his power comes, you can have patience with joy, which is the best kind.

This very hope gives us cause to be thankful unto the Lord because He lets us have fellowship with great Christians like you. This is possible only because God has delivered us from all evil influences and placed us in the middle of God's Christly kingdom. It is, after all, through Christ that we have the assurance of salvation and forgiveness because he gave up his life for us.

Christ is an exact copy of God himself, the first one made of all that is made. Christ made all of reality, whether we can see it or not. Christ made all that is good and evil. All reality exists for Christ's benefit. This is because Christ was before all else. He is now the great adhesive of the universe.

10
From the "Lesser" to the Least

The books of the New Testament not called "gospels" or not attributed to the pen of Paul hold great truths applicable to modern missions. They are not "lesser epistles" in the sense of being unimportant to modern disciples.

One outstanding example of this fact is the short but significant book of Jude. This book is important because it points to the relation between what faithful Christians say they believe and what they do. In a day in which outsiders look to the church for hope, ethical behavior is essential. If a missionary's mouth talks the talk but his feet do not walk the walk, there is trouble.

The author of this little book was probably Jude, the half-brother of Jesus (about AD 80). The whole purpose is to refute an early heresy called gnosticism.

After a brief greeting, Jude appeals for a common belief in orthodox faith designed to mold Christians together amidst heresy all around them. Jude makes it clear that he is willing "to contend" or fight as in military warfare to preserve the faith. That faith he wants to protect is a body of Christian beliefs worth dying and fighting for. These truths for Jude are so central to the faith that they can be said to be eternal. The early church did not waste any time getting such beliefs together and codifying them in forms for which they would fight. This certainly encouraged the leaders to see themselves as having authority. Therefore, anyone who did not agree with these early doctrinal statements was described as an antiauthoritarian radical.

Those who rebelled against the Christian faith were called murmurers, complainers, self-willed, people who talked too much without thinking about what they were saying. Their life-style of unethical behavior will lead, Jude assured them, to an even more corrupt life.

The last half of the little letter of Jude is a passionate appeal to the loyal. Jude asks them to pray according to the will of the Holy Spirit. This act alone, Jude promised, would keep the faithful immersed in the mercy and love of God. The result was bound to be the quality of life only to be called eternal.

The beautiful doxology with which Jude concludes is the most memorized portion of it. The readers were promised that God could keep them from falling. Jesus the Christ is listed here as Lord, more than a Savior. Jude seemed to be reaching for all the words he could muster. He gave to God "glory, majesty, dominion, and eternity" not only in time past and time to come, but now.

Jude stands as a constant reminder to modern missionaries that correct doctrine is of prime importance to God's kingdom. There is no room for theological fuzziness or sloppiness for those who see themselves as proclaiming the truth. Christian apologists will be needed in the future even more than now as attacks come from various sources against Christian teachings.

Second Peter barely made it into our Bible. Modern missionaries should be glad it did. The book is obviously written to combat the heresy of gnosticism that plagued the first-century church. The reader then and now is also reminded that Christ will one day return to earth to triumph in glory. The author calls for the growth of every Christian into true knowledge. That true knowledge, according to Peter, is the method by which God saves the entire person, not merely his soul. The Gnostics maintained that since flesh is evil, God only wants to save the soul.

According to Peter, when the believing Christian understands that he is to grow in completeness toward God and personal development, there are definite characteristics he is to display. The first of these is love, which serves as a strong foundation. The second is faith which joins love in that strong foundation. The third component is virtue, which is another way of saying integrity which the world seeks. That moral excellence which the Christian can display only through the Holy Spirit is the basic quality of life-style that can make the gospel attractive in any culture.

Veteran missionaries report that numerous converts come in the last years of their ministry because the people observe that there is a basic agreement between their words and their life. Here that is called virtue. There is no substitute for it in missionary service. To virtue the believer should add knowledge, which is practical application of theology. There is a practical bent to the gospel. It has always been more than a mere theory about the heavens. Knowledge helps make that good news livable. The next is self-control. More than one missionary has returned sadly from the field because of a sexual taboo broken or an indiscretion. The Greek word used here is almost always used in relation to controlled sexual expression.

The next characteristic of the true believer is steadfastness. The Greek word means literally to stand up under a heavy burden. No matter how the word *burden* is translated here, missionaries understand it. The burden may be economic, physical, medical, loneliness, or psychological. Only the Lord can help the believer carry such loads. The believer acknowledges that fact and that within itself lightens the load. The next is godliness, which is best understood to mean reflecting accurately the image of God. Christians are mirrors of the divine, not self-starters within themselves. The final one listed is brotherly love, which is the earthly expression of the heavenly love God initiated in Christ. All these add up to form the effective disciple who reflects God's good news.

In 2 Peter 1:16 he reminded his readers that his teaching was not based on "cunningly devised myths." This was an obvious reference to the Gnostics, who claimed an exclusive hold on truth not available to the lowly common believer. Rather, Peter based his testimony on the transfiguration of Jesus of which he was an eyewitness. That was Peter's foreknowledge of what Jesus' second coming will be like. Modern missionaries will run into any number of strange views of how humans are to find God. They may range from bowing before a shrine to beating oneself with whips to speaking in tongues. The important point for the missionary to remember is that his testimony is based on this past, present, and future experience of Christ. Peter saw Christ transfigured. Each of us who claims the title missionary have a time to draw on when we first saw Christ in proper perspective as Son of God. We also have the present reality of Jesus in our total being. This is coupled with the hope of Jesus' return. All of this the Holy Spirit combines to equip us to say that Jesus is the way to find God.

Peter went on to say that our knowledge of God in Christ is based on Holy Scripture. Here he assumes the vital inspiration of Scripture. Just as the Holy Spirit was directly involved in giving Scripture to the original authors, he is today allowing inspired disciples to discern its meaning. This is great comfort to the ambassadors for Christ who preach the Word. They can rest assured that the truths found in the Scriptures are valid for their hearers. All hesitancy vanishes when this fact is grasped. It is God's Word which reaches their hearers, not the cunning craftiness of a few witty sages.

Chapter 2 of 2 Peter is given to a description of false teachers claiming to be Christian. This description may be seen as the opposite of the true teacher for Christ. Note that not only was what they taught false, they were themselves of false character. Because their inner being was corrupt, their teachings were false. False doctrine and false character were combined to make them doubly dangerous. The end result is their own destruction as well as the hearers to whom they spoke.

The false teachers, first-century Gnostics, were marked by greed. They exploited their very hearers by a kind of verbal diarrhea in which their listeners were soon caught up in false greed as well. Peter prophesied that they would soon be eaten alive by their own deception. Their hearers would soon catch on to their inherent wickedness and turn on them with the destructive powers they had learned so well from these false teachers. These false and morally corrupt teachers can be assured of their impending destruction only by studying history. God did not even spare his beloved angels who rebelled against him. The angels were cast into hell. The plight of the false teachers will be even worse.

Further, God did not spare the wicked world in Noah's day. The waters came in spite of Noah's preaching of righteousness. Sodom and Gomorrah were destroyed in spite of the pleas of Lot. The false teachers can expect their final lot to be even worse than the fire rained down on these two evil cities.

Peter continued by describing the false teachers as so presumptuous as to stand with their corruption in the face of God and godly people. They had no shame in their filthy deeds. They were called willful, determined to go to their own destruction in spite of the certain consequences. They were also outright blasphemers who publicly put the name of God to scorn. Peter called them stupid animals who make animalistic sounds without regard for cohesiveness in their sayings. They are described as so blatant in their sin that they make those animal noises in open daylight. In a most obvious image, Peter described these enemies of the true gospel as waterless clouds who seem to promise rain but cannot deliver. They think they are free but they are slaves indeed to their own ungodliness. Their own destruction is inherent within their own teachings. The true teacher, on the other hand, is destined to be blessed of God because of his faithfulness to the truth. He has not sought to delude the people but has tried to lead the hearers based on truth found in the inspired Holy Scripture. The result is that their followers live lives of joy and anticipation of a great knowledge of Christ when he returns. They are objects of God's love, not his powerful wrath seen at Sodom and Gomorrah.

The final chapter of 2 Peter stressed the great joy coming to true followers of Christ at his second coming. He warned against "scoffers" who were teaching that Jesus would not return. These false teachers argued that things would continue just as they always had. There was no reason, they counseled, to await any big change. With God, Peter argued, time is not calculated in the same way humans do it. "One day is as a thousand years," Peter argued. This should stand as a warning to those living two thousand years after the first coming of Christ that careful calculations of God's timetable is an impossible task for mere humans. So far everyone who has set the date for the return of Christ has been wrong.

It is the missionary's role to remind his subjects that their faith is in a returning Savior, not a scheme. But, some learn slowly, and the cause of missions is still likely to be hurt by some who are more concerned with predicting than with service. Peter's argument was that it is God's grace that has kept him from sending Christ. He still desires that all come to repentance. Those who note that Jesus has not returned should not be lulled to sleep. God will bring this present order to an end, in his own good time and for certain! This present world is not even designed to last forever. It will one day be replaced by a kingdom of peace and complete righteousness. The missionaries of today can bank on that fact. We are not dealing with only timely truths but also timeless. Eternal life is designed basically for eternity. This present order is living on borrowed time due only to God's patience. This gives the messenger a great sense of urgency about the task.

Peter concludes this short book by calling for expectant and holy living. This holiness should be combined with evangelism. It is not a head-in-the-sand holiness designed to save and preserve self, but on outgoing concern for holiness in all of society. This is possible when all grow in that powerful combination of grace and knowledge. This will ensure a people ready to greet Jesus with joy on his return. This little letter closes by praising Christ and reminding the readers that he is the Lord of both now and the future.

Hebrews is the most practical book outside the Gospels in the New Testament as far as modern application of the gospel is concerned. The images used therein are those understood quite well by most people in Third World countries today. Those familiar with the barter system of trade, with the sacrifice of animals, and with religious festivals can identify with the pictures of Christ found in Hebrews. It is a natural point-of-contact for those in the western world wanting to bring the gospel to others in terms they can understand.

The fact that the author cannot be known for sure does not diminish its worth. The letter was probably written about AD 82 by an author in the middle of a persecution, probably the Domitian one. The original audience was probably a group of persecuted Jewish Christians in Rome.

The letter was written to a group of second-generation Christians who had some problems common to secondhand believers. One

was ritual formalism. Worship had degenerated into the rigid fulfillment of a set of rites. The second problem in this group is that of
overfamiliarity with Christian doctrine. They were tending to take
certain things for granted. They were both spiritually and intellectually stagnant. This resulted in spiritual apathy. The apathy led
to ethical and moral compromise. They were behaving in the same
manner as their pagan neighbors. The author accuses his readers of
crucifying Jesus afresh in their pagan morality. Worse than that,
they are treading their Savior under their feet as if he is useless
trash.

What the author of Hebrews said is still relevant in today's
church. A basic recurring problem is static apathy. This can happen
so easily when the first generation of believers is gone. There is
something inherently firsthand about the gospel. One knows Christ
intimately or not at all. The missionary today can tend to grow
stagnant. His new converts can serve to remind him that there is a
daily freshness in the gospel itself. This contact can lead to a renewed self-commitment. This daily renewed dedication can serve to
combat the influence of a pagan society which wants to take the
sting out of the gospel. The author reminds the modern reader that
all truth is in Christ. By focusing only on him, the new and old
believers can retain the freshness and authenticity of the gospel.

The first four verses of Hebrews are a clear statement of God's
effort to reveal himself to all peoples. God is and God has spoken.
These are the presuppositions of the Hebrews writer. Later he will
say that what God has said partially in the prophets, he has said
fully in Jesus of Nazareth. Christianity is, more than any other religion, a religion of revelation. His revelation comes clearest through
humans. Formerly he used prophets. Now Jesus replaces that
method of revelation. Jesus does not belong among the list of
prophets. He is in a category all by himself, in spite of what Islamic
people say. They have Jesus as only one of a long list of prophets.
In Jesus we find the bearer of eternal life, not a mere announcer of
truth.

Jesus is unique, according to the Hebrews writer, in four ways:

1. *He is the heir of all things.*—The author is saying here that

Jesus is the fulfillment of all other revelation. As the heir of all godly searching for humans in the past, Jesus is now at the right hand of the Father serving as our divine representative.

2. *Jesus is the Creator of all things.*—The miracle of Jesus is that the very one who made us later became one of us. Christ made us and then remade us through the doorway of the empty tomb.

3. *Jesus reflects the glory of God.*—Jesus came to earth as the exact image of the heavenly Father. He is the facsimile of God. If anyone would know the Father, he should look at the Son.

4. *Upholding the universe.*—For Paul, "in him all things hold together" (Col. 1:17, RSV). The author of Hebrews puts Christ's role in an even more important place. It is he who is the foundation, not only of missions, but of the entire universe.

These four qualities listed above are in the present tense. Christ is able to do all these four works, according to this introduction to Hebrews, because he has earned that right by doing three things. First, Christ was made a purifying factor for our sins. This made much-needed forgiveness possible for all in the human family. Second, he sits at the right hand of the Father. Christ's fleshly work is completed. His role can never be challenged. Third, Jesus has been made higher than the angels. The original readers believed that they were surrounded by angels. That view predominates in most cultures today. To present Christ as being equal to the High God and above all spirit beings is a bragging point often missed by Western-minded missionaries. Again Hebrews comes through as a natural vehicle for communicating the gospel.

Hebrews 4:14-16 presents Jesus as the greatest of all high priests. This imagery is readily understood by most people in the world because they are familiar with "witch doctors" and priests in small bush villages. In the old days, the primary function of the priest was the hearing of confession. There is no greater need for modern man than the removal of guilt. The author of Hebrews presents us with the powerful idea that the very priest who takes our confession is the same one who hears it. Jesus is able to fulfill that role because he is perfect. He is in constant touch with God because of his very nature. By being who he is, Jesus brings God to man and vice versa.

Jesus understands the plight of being human because he has gone through every possible temptation that we go through. No missionary has ever been lonelier or more frustrated or more hurt than Jesus has already experienced. The result of this realization is that we can all now go right up to the throne of grace and anticipate full understanding and forgiveness with never any fear of rejection. That makes modern prayer an exercise in positive reinforcement.

Hebrews 6:1-12 is the most eloquent call in the Bible for doctrinal and spiritual maturity. The call is for Christians to leave behind "elementary doctrines" and grow toward spiritual maturity. Unfortunately, there are many born-again Christians who remain year after year in the kindergarten of Christian growth. They pile elementary points up without ever moving on to stronger and deeper doctrine.

The author of Hebrews lists six doctrines which are absolutely essential. First, there is turning away from a self-destructive life-style. The word which applies here may be called repentance. Second, there is the fundamental doctrine of the role of Christ in forgiving sins. Third, there is the basic experience of faith. Without faith, the Christian life cannot begin or continue. Fourth, there is baptism, done in obedience to the command and example of Christ. Fifth, there is the dominant fact of the Christian life-style in Pauline theology, the resurrection of Jesus. Finally, there is the final judgment which serves as a daily reminder that we are responsible for our attitudes and actions.

The point of this entire section is that all six of these doctrines are essential, but baby food. Jesus never intended for his followers to spend their time mastering these six without growing any more toward other truths. Some missionaries make the mistake of making their teachings to new converts so basic that they ignore deeper growth. The author then makes the point that if they desert Jesus, they crucify him afresh. Those who refuse to grow or leave Jesus out of their lives are nailing his hands to a modern and daily cross.

Hebrews 7:26-28 portrays Jesus as the perfect High Priest. He is presented as "holy and blameless"; that is, he never even made a mistake when on earth in fleshly form. He never harbored any bad attitudes. Jesus was appointed as a perfect priest to bring our sins far away from us. Having done that, he rules as our permanent priest. Our salvation is the result of the continuous activity of God in Christ. It is Christ who alone is the Son of God and God, King, Judge, and High Priest perpetually.

Hebrews 11 defines faith by example for the readers. This is the most classic definition of faith found anywhere in the Bible. Missionaries discover quickly the truth stated here; that is, faith is not a call to laziness but to action. Faith is not a Pollyanna daydream of what could be. It is the believer betting his life that God really exists. It is the realization that God's best blessings still await us even when the light seems dimmest. All of this is based on the insight that both the present and the future belong to God. This is because the Christian understands that God made everything in the past (v. 3). Faith is a contract based on contact between God's revelation and our heart.

The author then calls the roll of great persons of the Hebrew Scriptures who showed great faith. All of them discovered that faith never seeks God in vain. In fact, God seeks us before we ever turn to him. Noah is one of the most important listed here. Noah was a man who cared not what others thought. Building an ark before the first raindrop took a great measure of faith. Noah was pronounced guilty of premature morality by his peers. But, his faith allowed him to see the future. He knew his faith would be rewarded in his own lifetime.

The greatest example in this faith chapter is Abraham. He believed in God before anyone in his generation even knew who God was. His belief was strong enough to send Abraham out to a country unheard of among his peers. Abraham risked the venture of plunging into the unseen. When he arrived at the land promised to him, it was as a stranger. Every missionary, home or foreign, knows that feeling. To be on the move with the gospel is to live in a land made strange by one's frame of reference. The believer relates to the God of the future. This allows him to see things above and beyond the crowd. Sometimes the life of faith is a lonely existence, but God is there giving hope and patience. Abraham existed on faith because he knew there was something beyond this life which

God was calling him to. The ultimate test came when he was asked to give up Isaac. Isaac was the one concrete sign of the promise God had made to him that he would bless all nations. At the last minute God saved Isaac. Abraham's faith had proven adequate to the test. Many a missionary has walked away from a difficult situation not leaving behind any physical sign that God had given. But years later his work has paid off when God honored his faithful service. The principle of God's taking note of an ambassador's faithfulness is still true today.

The first two verses of Hebrews 12 is built on the great roll call of the faithful found in the preceding chapter. It is clear here that one never has faith in isolation. The race of life is never run in an empty stadium. The "home crowd" advantage is always with the faithful. We are being cheered on by those in the past who watch us from their reserved seats on high. Abraham, Noah, and Moses watch as we seek others who see the value of faith in God. Since we are being watched by past giants of faith, it is foolish for us to try to run in embarrassment to ourself with the heavy weight of sin around our ankles. This would be as foolish as an Olympic runner competing with the training weights still on his ankles. The "sin which clings" is a veiled reference to the warmup robe used by first-century runners. Running the race of life fully robed would be foolish. The men like Abraham who watch would laugh at our foolishness.

A phrase which captured the general public in the 1970s was "the loneliness of the long distance runner." There is a sense in which faith keeps a missionary going in the midst of loneliness. That faith comes only through self-control. Perserverance is the most required characteristic of a runner and of a missionary. The ribbon at the end of the race leads to Jesus. The successful runner is the one who looks to nothing or no one except Jesus. The obstacles and distractions along the way call to the runners. Some stop for what they think is a moment and it turns into a lifetime. Others go on, "despising the shame" itself. They are deaf to ridicule and security because they know the awaiting crown of Christ is worth the cost. They are self-controlled and self-denied through the Spirit who grants them faith.

The last chapter of Hebrews is a call to essential Christian virtue or integrity. It is a counsel on Christian ethics. The first verse is a reminder of the importance of "brotherly love." There is nothing so sad as for a Christian to desert or be deserted by his fellow believers. No one ever goes alone to God. There is a sense in which we only find God when we find each other. To ignore that fact of Christian existence is to limp along crippled by unconcern. The Hebrews author is saying that, at whatever cost, the believer should give priority to having strengthening fellowship with his brother and sister believers.

Verse 2 takes that concern one step further. The Christian is to be known not only as one who loves the brothers, but as one who loves the unbelievers. Many a missionary has failed at one or both of these tasks. He had not been able to work with other members of his mission or has failed to show aggressive love to those outside the church. To fail in either place is to cripple the cause of Christ. The reference to "angels unawares" was probably originally describing Christian messengers who had no money to pay for lodging. But, the idea of real angels is an intriguing one. The "least of these" applies here. Every undernourished baby, leper, hungry teenager, or sick father cared for by a loving Christian counts the same with God as serving one of his favorite angels. God in Christ showed a definite concern for the oppressed of all kinds.

There are more kinds of prisons than those with iron bars. Modern humans are imprisoned by religions, political, and educational systems. The Christian is called to break down those systems. At times it is just as Christian to protest rent increases to those with fixed incomes as it is to pass out gospel tracts. The Lord God honors setting at liberty the captives from whatever the source of bondage.

The author then mentions the importance of maintaining Christian homes. More effective long-range ministry and witness has been by missionaries through the maintenance of a good and stable Christian home than by any other method. This is done partly through healthy and pure sexual expression. There is no downplaying of the role of sex here. It is to be kept under control. Another issue is listed next. The faithful believer is to stay clear of the love of money. Money and sex misused have ruined many an otherwise effective missionary. The missionary is paid in wages eternal and he is to be content with what he has. A corollary is that one is to rejoice in the daily provisions God makes. The paragraph closes with the promise that makes the practice of Christian virtue possible; that is, God will never disappoint or abandon the faithful. As a missionary manual on personal faith and transcultural communication images, the book of Hebrews is unsurpassed in the New Testament.

The so-called "Lesser Epistles" in the New Testament are packed with diamonds of truth for the serious yet joyous missionary of today. There is nothing minor about them in their value for the clear witness to a searching world.

ADDENDUM
Paraphrase of James 1:1-11

My name is James. Jesus and I grew up in our father Joseph's carpenter shop. Now Jesus is my Lord as well as my half-brother. I am writing this letter to all Christians everywhere and in every age.

My good friends in the Lord, clap your hands in gladness when you have irritations because these just serve to make you stronger believers. One day you'll be much stronger than you are now if you don't let little things bother you.

If any one of you wants to know more about anything, pray about it. God will then reveal mysteries to you which only prayer can make known. The way to learn is to ask in full faith with no room for doubting. Anyone who prays while doubting is like an ocean wave which disappears in an instant when it gets to the shore. It may look powerful for a moment, but it soon vanishes. Praying with both faith and doubt is like trying to drive two automobiles at once. One or both of them will run off the road.

If you are poor, think of the good things you have. Take none of them for granted. If you are rich, always realize that your so-called riches can pass away like dry grass in a wild prairie fire. A rich person can be eaten up, if he is not careful, by his own love of money. The beauty is soon gone. What really lasts is dependence on God in faith.

11
Future Hope of John

The last book in the Bible is one of a type, including also Daniel. The word most often used to describe this type is "apocalypse." This type of literature appeared in Bible days during periods of great stress brought about by a foreign power. The message is always the same: those who persevere during persecution will be rewarded by God later. The purpose of the writer of apocalypse literature is always to explain and justify the dealings of God when it appears that he has deserted the faithful.

Revelation, like other apocalypses, is characterized by strange and mysterious figures, usually seen in visions and explained by angels.

The Revelation of John claims to have Jesus as its author and the apostle John as his recorder. The entire book is obviously Jesus himself revealing himself to a faithful prophet. The message is one of peace for those under great persecution by the Romans. The first readers of the Revelation knew persecution from two sides; pious Jews and Roman political figures. The emperor worship of the Romans was one which was by definition anti-Christian. The emperors insisted that temples be built to their honor and some of them liked the title, "Lord and God."

This was sheer blasphemy to the believer in Christ. Christians were being cut off from political and economic advantages unavailable to them as anti-Roman. Further, they were not even allowed to live simple lives unpersecuted. All the empire was watching the new Christian church and their reaction to persecution would be counted for or against their Master. During these times they knew the value of the perpetual presence of Christ, but life was still difficult under the pagan Romans. They looked to the skies for the return of Christ and were growing impatient and disappointed when he did not come. In the middle of all this, there were the temptations of sinful and fleshly Roman values on an everyday basis.

To these persecuted Christians, John wrote the good news that God was still on his throne and very much in control of worldly affairs. John presented God as much stronger than Satan. It was his message that the ultimate victory over Satan has already been won by the death and resurrection of Christ. Soon, and very soon, Christ would establish his rule right among the Romans. The believers could bet their lives on that fact. A result of all this would be a new Jerusalem, in which there would be no reason for fear.

This message was originally designed to give encouragement to some brave folks who needed to be even bolder in the midst of persecution. The practical application was that the Christians were to bear up bravely under their perils and pains. Their model was Jesus, who has already endured under severe persecution. Christ demonstrated that death was not defeat for him or his followers. Those who could stay with him would be rewarded with the same type of life and victory.

Revelation has historically been interpreted four main ways. One is to see the book as symbolic of a fight between principles here on earth. Evil and good are warring and all of us are battlegrounds for that war, according to this view. So, for example, the new Jerusalem is seen as symbolic of the daily victory won by faithful Christians. A second view is to see Revelation almost purely in the sense of the past tense as a commentary on the way things used to be under the Romans. A third method, a popular one, is to see the entire history of the church in the book. All the symbols are freely interpreted to apply to various stages of church history. A final way is to see the entire book as predicting the future. This futurist method has predominated in evangelical Christianity, often to the extent that the book loses much of its present punch. This is especially tragic in its application toward missions because today's warriors need the same kind of encouragement that the early Christians did. They live under dire circumstances, often in situations where they are not welcome. Especially in Islamic and Communist nations, these modern martyrs must work under severe persecution. They deserve to know that the visions of John are just as meaningful today as in the first century.

The author was the apostle John while in exile on the isle of Patmos. His teachings are essentially the same as those found in the Gospel of John. These include the emphasis on a continuing battle between good and evil, light and darkness. Another similarity is the emphasis on Christ's humanity and redemptive work through the cross. Also evident is an emphasis in both books on Christ's divine power.

The first three chapters of the Revelation are composed of a vision by John of the Son of man (an obvious reference to Christ as this is one of John's favorite ways to refer to him). In this vision John is commanded to write to seven churches. When we read them today, they read as if written to us in person. Immediately John identifies the entire book as a vision given by Christ. Christ is the true author. John makes this clear early. The salutation (v. 1:4-8) of the first chapter is a summary of the book's themes: the power of God, the available energy of the Holy Spirit, and the active redeeming lordship of Christ. In other words, the persons of the Trinity are very much in control of events for their believers.

In verse 8, the speaker is referred to as the Alpha and the Omega. These are the first and last letters of the Greek alphabet. In verse 18, Jesus speaks as the one who lives eternally. This gives him an overview of history that the poor pilgrim does not have. It is Jesus, we are to remember, who has the keys to all of history. In every time and place, Jesus is the Lord of all events.

Chapter 2 begins the letters to the seven churches. Seven is the perfect number and the seven churches represent all the churches of all ages. The main purpose of all seven letters is to give encouragement to all churches to pass victoriously through all its trials. The enemies are presented as threefold: false teaching, pious Jews, and powerful Roman conquerors. The readers are told not to take part in heathen festivals around them and to keep themselves pure from pollution of any kind.

The first letter is to Ephesus, a church blamed because its first love has cooled. That dilemma is still a modern problem. The loss of fervor often happens so slowly that it is gone before the believer notices it. Today, the workaholic missionary must guard against the slow loss of his reason for being on the field. Only daily discipline and openness to Christ can keep fervor from slowly seeping away. Fervor goes hand in hand with love. Gradually Ephesus Christians had lost their love and were worthy only of being destroyed. Service without love is useless.

The second letter is to Smyrna. There is no condemnation for this church. It is praised for its endurance of persecution and poverty. This is in spite of the fact that a few so-called Jews are among them trying to draw them away from a freedom-giving gospel. They are being used of the devil, according to John, to try to draw believers into the trap of legalism. Because of their faithfulness, the Symrna Christians were not to be led astray.

The third is the church in Pergamum. They are warned against being led away by immoral teachers. They have given in somewhat by following after the flesh and are urged to repent. The image of the sword is used to describe Christ's power, stronger by far than anything Rome has to offer. If they remain true in spite of persecution, the Christians in Pergamum will get a "new name." All the early readers recognized this symbol as one of new life in Christ, a reality not accessible to Roman power.

The church in Thyatira is condemned for harboring corrupt teaching. It is noteworthy here that individual believers are asked to be faithful even when the majority are not. This, however, is presented in the balanced view that the church is the collective body of Christ. Only when the church is badly corrupted are individual members to act independently of the body. Today it is the persons who love the church most deeply who are most critical of it. It is not unchristian to be critical of the church when it is going against the claims of Christ. Missionaries in a mission meeting sometimes have to speak prophetically in spite of the majority rule. Thyatiran Christians are also asked not to follow after Jezebel, a symbol of pagan rituals used by the Romans including illicit sexual practices. There was the flesh on one side and false teaching on the other. Some were pretending to teach the "deeper things" of God while leading the believers away from God. Missionaries today have to be constantly on the alert against heresy, often coming even from well-meaning but immature Christians. The teaching role of the missionary is never completed. There is no let up when examining the implications of the gospel. Those who remain faithful will see the glory of Christ as the Morning Star. But, this new day free from persecution is only for those who remain free from heresy and the lust of the flesh.

The letter to the church in Sardis begins the third chapter of Revelation. There is no praise for this church because it lives out of touch with spiritual reality. It is spiritually dead but has the power to be awakened. This is because there are a few faithful ones even in this dead church. These few faithful will one day receive their robes, symbolic of their purity.

The letter to the church in Philadelphia is a jewel. Some of the unfaithful Jews who had been guilty of aiding the Romans in persecution were converted through a few faithful believers. Let every missionary who ever wanted to give up under pressure note this example. Every one who persecutes takes a jab and backs off to see how the victim will react. Those who react in love will win and even the persecutors know that fact. The orthodox Jews were at that time strong in Philadelphia. They regarded the new Christians as an enemy and a threat at first but were beginning to give the gospel a chance when they watched the true believers turn the other cheek.

The final letter was directed to the church at Laodicea. The church was not without blame and its sins were chiefly three: being lukewarm, self-satisfaction, and worldliness. These three, according to Christ through John, are basically due to trusting in self instead of Christ. Christ is now whipping Laodicea, the letter states, because he loves the church dearly. It needs zeal and repentance. It is to this lukewarm church that Jesus appeals by standing outside and knocking at the doors of their collective hearts. The irony is that due to their self-centeredness, Christ is standing outside his own church. Christ feels like spewing them out of his mouth but remains patient.

His patience, John says, will one day pay off because he will be host at a giant feast where his guests will be the faithful ones.

Today's missionaries are pressured by the same lukewarmness which ate away from the inside of first-century Christians. The only antidote is a constant mindfulness that Christ is the only authentic source for inner assurance and power.

Revelation 4 follows up on the seven letters. Here now the faithful are presented the image of God and the Lamb. The powers of Christ are exalted and powers of evil are seen in ignoble defeat. God is pictured as sitting on his heavenly throne surrounded by ministering angels. He lives "above the water floods." The sea was never understood by the Hebrews. They feared it greatly. God was therefore seen as sitting above the sea as a symbol of victory over the stormy persecutions underneath his feet. The readers are reminded that their persecutors were created by the heavenly Father and exist only because God allows, but does not condone, their temporary activity. Every missionary who fears an unruly chief or a gang leader in a ghetto should remember that God created even them. Therefore, the capacity for repentance is theirs and never impossible.

Chapter 5 of the Revelation presents the glory of Christ. John sees the roll of a book which symbolizes the full contents of God's purposes for the future. The message is clear: the future belongs only to God and his people. Through the cross, the devil and worldly temptations have already been overcome. Now God's purposes can be worked out. The church will one day sing "Worthy is the Lamb." The chorus of praise will become universal. So, now every gospel hymn is but a foretelling of a universal choir that will one day sing praises to the one who will be our director. Every created thing will be in harmony with him.

Revelation 10 pictures a mighty angel with a small book in his hand. The crescendo of seven thunders introduces it. John is commanded to eat the book. It is sweet in his mouth but bitter in his stomach. This is symbolic of the fact that John's contact with God is sweet but the words are bitter due to present persecution. Any missionary or prophet knows the thrill of being close to God but the agony of having the message ignored or smashed by persecution. John knows, as even the faithful do today, that his task is an essential one if not always one of sweetness.

Revelation 12 discusses the persecution which the church had suffered and which is about to burst forth again. This chapter is a turning point. From now on the book will discuss the future triumph of Christ and his church. This chapter emphasizes the basic enemy of Christ, Satan. Satan is symbolized as polluted by the blood of the persecuted saints. The faithful Christians are pictured as pure and dressed in white. The church escapes from the blood-red dragon, aided by God in Christ. In verses 10-12, Satan is pictured as already defeated. The point is that Satan will never be able to harm the faithful portion of the church.

Revelation 14 pictures the blessedness of those who witness a true confession of Christ and harsh judgment on the ungodly. The chapter opens as Jesus pictured as a Lamb on Mount Zion, the true picture of the perfect number in the faithful church. One-hundred forty-four thousand is a symbolic number for the perfect number of the redeemed. The faithful are pictured as unmarked by idolatry and having confessed the true God and not the dumb and lying idols. Babylon is described as already fallen. Today's emissaries for Christ can securely operate on the premise that evil forces will be destroyed. They can operate as if this is already an accomplished fact. On the other hand, those who are not faithful to God will come under his wrath, a plight much worse than the persecution offered by the Romans.

Chapter 17 paints Rome as the great whore of Babylon. The Hebrews knew Babylon as the center of a world-power and the ancient and persistent enemy of God's people. Babylon was always feared by the Hebrews. (Note: not until the Persians overcame Babylon did the Jews get to return to Judah.) The last days of Rome were probably the most immoral in all of world history. Vast wealth was squandered in the most shameless wickedness. Their cruelty was shocking. When their pleasure pursuits were satisfied, the suicide rates increased. The masses of the people were wallowing in ignorance and poverty. They labeled the Christians as being responsible for the decline of the Roman Empire. Further, they were blamed for the great fire which burned much of Rome in AD 64. Christians were singled out for persecution. Some were even covered with oil and burned at night to light the emperor's gardens. The horrible persecutions were symbolic of a degenerating Rome.

Chapter 18 foretells the destruction of Rome. Before the fall, God's children are called out of Rome lest they fall with the resounding thud that will soon come. Those who go along with the pagan practices will die with those who persecute God's precious children.

In chapter 20 the final overthrow of Satan is predicted. The persecuted ones know that they will see their enemies overthrown by the world's strongest force, God. God is seen as setting on a great white throne, an obvious symbol of power and purity. From there he destroys death by sending it to a bottomless pit; that is, as far away as even imagination can concoct.

Chapter 21 pictures the beautiful holy city. The judgment is over. One meaning is clear: all peoples, both Jews and Gentiles, are God's people now. This removes all distinctions between white American missionaries and "colored" Third World peoples. God desires all people to be his and dwell in his holy city. (Note: all things are new and free from pain, including the elements of creation.) Included also is a new society. The new walls represent beauty and security. The magnificent beauty of the city is symbolized by the most precious and expensive objects. There is no one in the new city who does not worship God in his life-style and value system. The full light and knowledge of God has overcome our current partial wisdom. No uncleanness is present. All persecution has ceased. Today's faithful missionaries can gain new insight and energy by dwelling in meditation on what it will be like someday, when all evil has vanished.

The final chapter in Revelation is a vision of the last day, with persecution ended. The inner life of the heavenly Jerusalem is described in full. In the new Jerusalem, life is restored to Eden's fullness. The redeemed offer up worship face to face with God. The key to the city is daily renewal and repentance. The final words in the book, as in all of history, are spoken by Christ himself. Those who are filled with faith will be filled with grace.

ADDENDUM
Revelation 22:12-21

Listen! All you who are faithful. I am coming very soon and I will have your reward right with me. All will be rewarded according to their works, not their fancy words. I am *A* and *Z* and all that comes between.

Happy is anyone who obeys my commandments because he will enjoy the fruits of his obedience. He can walk right in the gates of the most beautiful city ever. Those outside are worse than dumb animals, and are known today as fortune-tellers, pimps, murderers, whores, and they love lies.

I, Jesus, have sent angels to you to let you know these realities. I am the child of the favorite King David and the sunrise and sunset.

The Holy Spirit and the church both are inviting any who will to come to the holy city. I want anyone who is thirsty to come and drink the cool water of eternal life.

I am Jesus and I want it understood that anyone who adds to this written witness will die. Anyone who erases any of these words will perish as well. Also he will not stand a chance for that eternal quality of life.

I am Jesus and I say I am coming back to earth in power very soon. So be it. Come on down, Jesus!

May the presence of God be with all who read and heed this book. May it always be so!

12
Future Doings

Sweeping changes await the missionary of the twenty-first century. As the foundation for missions, Christ can provide impetus and inspiration for reacting redemptively to such changes as long as those changes are anticipated, analyzed, and met with affirmation, not fear.

As we have seen in previous chapters in this book, the Bible is filled with encouragement and emphasis on called persons going forth to spread God's good news. In the age of the patriarchs, the prophets, the intertestamental period and the early church, God called and sent out ambassadors in his name. It is certainly true that the early church saw the sending of messengers as a vital part of its obligation to God. That call was soon separated from mere Jewishness and became inclusive of all peoples. Their role was made even more difficult because the early church had few economic resources. It was not a high prestige group, but struggled for status in the Roman Empire. The result was a highly successful series of preaching and teaching campaigns that put the church on the map. But, all of that is past tense.

Today the Bible comes alive when we come to it. When we do, we bring whatever we have to the reading of the Bible. When we open the Bible, there begins a divine-human encounter. God reveals truth for missions in the process by reaching out to us through his inspired written Word. But we are involved also in that miraculous process. In order for the Bible to become the written Word for us, we must bring to it a submission of spirit, to be judged by it. The written Word is therefore alive when God allows us to come to it with our anxieties, shortcomings, frustrations, and desires for fulfillment. This encounter is a beautiful thing God allows all of us to be ourselves in all our potentiality. We find our own being by losing it in the written Word, later in service to other human beings, and to the world which God so dearly loves.

In the Bible, we see a God of involvement and revelation. We find God there, not sitting out in space contemplating his creation. Instead, we find him interacting with human beings, the same ones created for fellowship with God in the first place. So, Bible study for missions' sake becomes an exciting adventure because there is no attempt to hide the divine-human element in the Scripture. So, we see faithful Noah not only hammering wooden nails, but also lying naked and drunk after the Flood. We see David, not only riding triumphantly into Jerusalem, but also involved in adultery and murder. Yet, through all of this, we still find a caring God.

In Bible study it is important to keep a healthy balance between the three tenses—past, present, and future. To forget one in Bible interpretation is to do injustice to the other two. It is important to ask the original context of any verse, what it means today and what it may mean while serving the Lord of tomorrow.

Applying this method, let us look into the future of missions. This will help us in not dismissing the Bible as an outdated and irrelevant book. We can see its principles and ideals as applicable to today and tomorrow.

One such principle we can see in the Bible is that missions is related to the church. Worship and missions go hand in hand in the Bible. Divine conduct is directly related to human conduct throughout the Bible. A major emphasis based on that fact is that we are above all in life to do the will of God. This is because we are made in God's image and we are fully human in direct proportion to the way we reflect our built-in godlikeness. Throughout the Bible God is presented as loving, just, merciful, righteous, and forgiving. So, we are to display those qualities in our life. All of this is based on the expression of love. Missions is the extension of love for God and love for neighbor. This involves forgiveness, compassion, and redeeming ministry to our neighbors. This love on the mission field is to be extended to other human beings without regard for their status or response. The love for God which thrusts one into missions involves trust and obedience. Love for neighbor is active goodwill. So, the two go together in missions.

The showing of love is possible because of the fellowship of faith called the church. It serves as the context of Christian prayer, worship, community, sharing, teaching and sending forth. This community meets around the lordship of Christ. It is in obedience to his person and teachings that we are told, "Go therefore and make disciples of all nations . . ." (Matt. 28:19, RSV). This is possible only in the living of the Spirit-filled life. Jesus has kept his promise when he said the Spirit would comfort, guide, and empower modern disciples. One of the things the Spirit has taught through the ages is that God is never a respector of persons in relation to wordly standards of status. The Spirit also monitors and empowers the moral life of the missionary.

Part of the mandatory mission task of the future is the cultivation of virtue and the elimination of vices on the part of the missionary. The well-being of every individual in the world is a vital concern to God. This will allow the Spirit-filled missionary to treat every human in the world with dignity and respect regardless of the cultural context. The missionary's interpersonal relations will continue to be important in future doings for missions. This basic fact will never be outmoded. Part of this responsibility is the caring for individuals (social ministry), and the evil social orders are to be challenged (social action). The demands for love in interpersonal relationships include social justice. This is especially true when systems crush widows and orphans. The future of missions is largely dependent on whether Jesus' voice is heard when he states that we will all be judged on whether we minister to needy persons. All of this demand for justice-oriented action in missions is highly dependent on our opinions and obedience. The Bible is for more than study. It demands service.

Modern missions are but a continuing part of a giant master plan to bring the world to the feet of Christ. This work encompasses all of time and space. Part of the bright future in missions will be based on a lessening of emphasis given to geography. It is the Bible's witness that all of life belongs to God. Realization of this fact in the future will help the task of missions.

It is as a kingdom of priests that the church can operate best in the future. This understanding will be aided further when we see that we operate in God's kingly court. All the world's a stage and God is the kingly director of the cosmic drama called life. Every actor called a missionary knows himself to be directly in touch with the director and commissioned by him to play a central role. Then are the missionary themes of the Bible fulfilled and the witnessing church can see that today and tomorrow's mission is a continuation of the personal work of Jesus. This is possible for tomorrow because of the reality of the resurrection of Jesus.

The future of missions is dependent on seeing that Pentecost (Acts 2) is not a once-for-all event. The sending of the Holy Spirit in power was the first sovereign act of the risen Lord. It was the great empowering of the entire church for worldwide witness. From that day forward, all are priests and prophets. This gives impetus to the modern idea that we are all missionaries. The selection of a few for extravagant commissioning services does not lessen the responsibility of any Christian for being an active missionary wherever he finds himself. Only in that reality can the church of the future hope to reach the entire world. The Holy Spirit thrusts all Christians into the world of different cultures and races for an ever-growing circle of witnesses. As this process grows, the world church becomes one of increasing richness and variety. The inclusion of all peoples into the church is a constant living reminder that the Christian mission is an ethical one. To be God's people on the march is to seek justice as well as individual salvation. The result will be that whole groups of people not currently interested in the gospel will respond in love because they have seen justice done.

The future of Christian missions stands waiting for those willing in Jesus' name to be more concerned about new dimensions of possibility than mourning over preserving lost truths. The pioneer spirit has always been, from the days of Abraham, a central theme of missions. First, it was geography that was explored as Paul and his various companions spread the gospel throughout the Roman Empire. Then the pioneer spirit was given to exploring Bible truths as second generation Christians sought to be as brave as their pioneering forefathers. Today there is much exploration of missionary methods as deep questions are asked about the best ways to reach the future world.

Missions in the future must explore the mystery in human variety on earth. This will help the American missionary drop his need to control. Missionaries who would be a sign of freedom available in the gospel must build the church on creative social patterns (such as cell groups for study) built on mutual respect rather than mistrust or competition or manipulation for control.

The Christian missionary of the future, in the Bible way, must offer worldwide support for the value of humans on two levels: a demand for repentance and a condemnation of any social structure not built on agape love. This can prevent Christian missions from becoming sentimental social service. Above all, the task of missions is a human one, based on the creativeness in life itself. The missionary operates from within the human family itself. In that spirit the next section is presented.

Eight Commandments for Future Missionaries

1. Keep up the basics.

Occasionally a fancy substitute is offered for Bible study and prayer but there is no such thing. The developing, well-balanced missionary of the future will be one in daily contact with his Creator and Commissioner.

2. Be as oblivious as possible to caste, status, and rank.

There will be no room in twenty-first century missions for any superior-inferior mentality, especially in light of Christianity's future growth outside the United States. Even a small vestige of a superior attitude on the part of any missionary can be crippling to those who are growing open to the Lord of the present and future.

3. Work out of a job with as much speed and depth as possible.

This means training national converts to replace missionaries as quickly as they are capable and willing. The Jesus model is clear here as we see him ascending to the Father and leaving the entire world with the disciples he spent so much time in training. Jesus did not hesitate in leaving the task of missions to the potentially weak disciples. This he did, knowing they would make serious and numerous mistakes. The open missionary of the future realizes that the national Christian knows more by accident about relating Christ to his culture than the foreign missionary can ever know on purpose.

4. Allow yourself to be ministered to in love.

The missionary of the future need not live in solitude. To be a missionary need not mean living constantly in total exhaustion by giving-giving-giving. Serious and comprehensive studies of why some missionaries of the past failed to show that they found no one in whom to confide and with whom to share joys and disappointments. When seen as loving pilgrims, national Christians can teach and console missionaries who are lonely. National Christians should be allowed to love missionaries without honoring them.

5. Immerse yourself as quickly and as thoroughly as possible into the culture to which you have been called.

The past mentality in which the missionary lived in the big house on the hill spoke loudly of status and separation. The Holy Spirit, who has the powerful capacity to break down walls, was given little chance to do so. Immersion into the lives of the nationals is a workable goal of the future.

6. Keep an "open-ended" view toward God's call.   Often missionaries feel trapped by a lifelong commitment to a specific decision made as a teenager. At retirement they emerge from their straitjacket as a free person, finally set free from a lifelong trapped feeling. It is true that God does occasionally call a person to one task for most of his life. However, it is never for the purpose of making a follower miserable. Flexibility helps overcome tedium, boredom, and hostility. God knows that. He may "recall" each one of us several times during our lifetime.

7. Equip others to be their best self.

The God of the future has not called us to be other than our best self. A complete takeover by Christ does not wipe out our personality but rather strengthens it. This can help us lose the tendency to dominate others when frustrated. God made us and wants us to be our very best self.

8. Be the best and call out the best.

Future missions, the work which is the apple of God's eye, deserves the best gifted and equipped of his saints. The best equipped in every local church should be asked the question constantly, "Why not missions for you?" Missionaries who are at their best set the model for those most gifted. This must mean that even in leisure hours allowing others to see Christian joy in every activity. The future demands the best of all of us.

New Frontiers

In the future, missions will be called upon to respond to such new frontiers as the population explosion, modern science, urbanization, society, leisure, and the aging.

Science today is providing for millions what religious truths have done in the past. It supplies a wide framework for insight underlying man's self-understanding. This insight, in turn, affects human activities, values, and hopes. The new scientism can only be met by aggressive missionaries who realize that science and the gospel often are seen as one package by the native Christian confronted by Americans in the name of Christ. This additional realization should also be coupled with the idea that science has become an alternative religion for many persons in the third world who have discovered in it a vehicle for achievement, status, and liberation. The future Christian response to science should include a retention of the sense of mystery and miracle. This should be combined with a celebration of the objectivity and openness with which science at its best approaches truth. This will allow Christianity and science to develop fully and in cooperation.

Computer technology can be a help to the future mission enterprise. Massive amounts of information can now be tracked as God goes where he wills. Missionaries can plan to be so flexible as to be where he is opening up human hearts to the gospel.

The whole communications explosion will continue to boom into the twenty-first century. Churches are expanding their ministries through video tapes, minicams, and cable television. Now even in small towns local churches can produce or purchase air time. By the year 2000 in the United States, the average American will have two thousand commercial messages beamed at him daily. He will be viewing an average of six hours daily. By that time, the average American youth who is graduated from college will have spent as much as 150 times watching television as in the classroom. Therefore, the church of the next century must be constantly aware of its image. Even more important, it is apparent that the gospel faces stubborn and well-financed competition for a hearing. Expert and visionary technicians in the mass media will be a must for the future.

Calcutta in 1981 is typical of the needs of the world's cities. There, one fourth of the food supply is consumed daily by rats. One half of the university students there are undernourished. Urbanization will be a dominant force in the next century. This will create severe identity crises in the lives of persons in the Third World as rural values are challenged. Those who combine Christian knowledge and love in these cities will be able to minister with meaning to those lonely in the crowd.

Mobility will be a major area of challenge to missions by the year 2000. By that time more than one third of all Americans will live outside the state of their birth. More than half of the American people changed residence between 1976 and 1981. The average American by the year 2000 will move sixteen times in his lifetime, compared with nine by Britons and six by Japanese. When adjustments to these moves are not properly made, crime rates rise, marriages are strained, racial and cultural clashes result, and divorce often occurs. Creative missionaries can see American mobility as a twofold opportunity. First, when American families move they are often open to receiving Christian ministry. Second, overseas residence for a few months can be made an option for lay missionaries willing to use their skills on a mission field.

The leisure revolution will continue to provide a backdrop for missions after AD 2000. In 1900 the work week in the United

States averaged sixty hours. In 1985 it will be thirty-four and is expected to average twenty-nine by 2000. In other words, the average American worker in 2000 will have three more years of leisure time in his lifetime than his great-grandfather had. Currently in the United States, 75 percent of all American free time is spent at home. Free time plus affluence has enabled many families to invest in boats and second homes. This continuing leisure revolution confronts Christian missions with two challenges: channeling the vast energy available through persons with time on their hands and creating innovative ministries to those in resort areas.

As life expectancy increases gradually around the world, the contribution of the elderly to missions can be tapped as a splendid source of labor. By 1985, the number of persons over sixty-five years of age in the United States will exceed 25 million. By 2001, that number is expected to total more than 33 million, or one in seven people. Most of them will be in good health physically, mentally, and spiritually. They will need to minister, not so much to be ministered to. Thus, they will constitute a vast reservoir of potential mission personnel. Futurizing in missions should properly include those elderly who can go on short-term junkets into their world to sink their best years in cultures foreign to their own.

These new frontiers offer a challenge to missions, but can be opportunities for greater service as long as they are anticipated, analyzed, and met with affirmation, not fear.

In structuring future missionary response to these areas of concern, certain Christian criteria should be kept central. They include:

1. *Strategic value.*—Missions in a rapidly changing world should be built on whether this task will affect an essentially significant group or power base. For example, a schoolteacher won to Christ can affect the lives of hundreds of parents and children over the decades.

2. *Economy.*—This factor will require well-trained eyes which can determine whether a specific mission activity will be effective in terms of receptiveness and resources. Great amounts of time and money have been almost wasted by dedicated persons who responded more to the romance than the advisability of doing missions in a certain time and place. The question of relating effect to

economic cost is the basic one for this standard.

3. *Instructive value.*—This factor will require well-trained eyes which can determine whether a specific mission activity will be effective in providing a pilot program for new patterns of mission-izing. The question is: Can this project be adequately evaluated so as to be instructive for others?

4. *Ecumenical cooperation.*—The question is: Will this strategy magnify the collective mission task of all the churches in the region? The divided groups of Christians today are being called of Christ to make Christ's desired unity a visible way of living and working together in his love. Every future missions plan ought to ask first whether it would glorify the Father better by including more of his children.

5. *Christian values.*—Justice, mercy, love for God and neighbor, and the servant quality of the Christian life must never be sold out to the spreading of a partial gospel polluted by the Western stand-ards of convenience and comfortable "soul-winning."

6. *Total world coverage.*—In 1981 certain geographical areas of the world are often described by missions experts to be "closed." Thus, the future demands more flexibility in mission planning and openness to persons who are by occupation businessmen, poli-ticians, doctors, and teachers making disciples by word and deed as they go.

7. *Integrity.*—This involves the avoidance of the use of deception, bribery, or intimidation to spread the gospel. It means the honesty to tell the truth about missions situations, other religions and denominations encountered there and telling about the real works and needs of the persons with whom we are ministering. This search for integrity avoids the use of any strategy making the objects of missions the victims of missionary pride, cunning, wealth, or cultural advantages. This task is timeless but a must for the future.

These seven criteria of future missions can keep evangelism cen-tered on both the least and best of God's children. These criteria, coupled with the goal of holistic redemption to all the human family, can aid all of us to reach our fulfillment in the saving work of Christ.

Hunger Pangs

Persons can hardly respond to the gospel if they are not alive. A mistake of the past cannot be repeated in the next century. Hungry people have been ignored except for their souls. By the year 2000 one person in four in the world will be suffering from hunger and/or malnutrition. This number will be almost two billion and each digit represents a real live human being. Nowhere in Scripture did Jesus command his followers to build buildings. If current trends continue, American Christians in 2001 will spend almost $20 billion on church construction alone. Futurizing by repeating past mistakes is to fail to learn. The Bible labels conscious neglect of the hungry as sin.

Conclusion

Positive missionizing of the future will continue to be based on premises and promises as old as creation. Biblical giants knew and taught that the justice which God requires is a justice of the market-places, the law courts, the palaces, and military juntas.

Jesus, in his first public sermon, quoted Isaish to set the tone for spiritual and social liberation. To ignore that truth in future mission-izing is to work off-center from Jesus' own ethical priorities.

Forgiveness and reconciliation can allow the oppressed and the oppressor alike to repent of the sin of the past and to plan together for hope in the future.

Jesus is the only legitimate foundation for missions. Only he can provide the power to react wholesomely to the problems of the future. That is because he is the Lord of yesterday, today, and for-ever.

ADDENDUM
Paraphrase of Revelation 21:1-8

And I saw a redeemed earth reflecting perfect heaven: all the old sinful standards were removed: and there was nothing left to fear.

Then I saw the new society, a new Jerusalem, sent by God and dressed in purity as a virgin bride.

Suddenly I heard a booming voice saying, "Listen! God wants to live among his human family and be their God as they are his obedient people."

And God will take away all our grief. Death will disappear and pain will be made harmless. All evil things will be a thing of the past.

The throne-dweller said, "Listen! It is I who have made all evil things harmless." He then said, "Write! What I am about to say is truth."

Then he said, "It is finished! I am *A* and *Z*. Anyone who is spiritually thirsty can come to me now. All who persevere will be entitled by faith for all these rewards. I will be their God and love them as my own dear children.

"But all cheaters, fearful, scoffers, murderers, pimps, fortune-tellers, liars, and idol worshipers shall fry in a lake of fire."